W. E. B. Du Bois and the
Critique of the Competitive Society

W. E. B. Du Bois and the Critique of the Competitive Society

ANDREW J. DOUGLAS

The University of Georgia Press   Athens

© 2019 by the University of Georgia Press
Athens, Georgia 30602
www.ugapress.org
All rights reserved
Set in Kepler by Melissa Buchanan

Most University of Georgia Press titles are
available from popular e-book vendors.

Printed digitally

Library of Congress Cataloging-in-Publication Data

Names: Douglas, Andrew J., 1980– author.
Title: W.E.B. Du Bois and the critique of the competitive society /
Andrew J. Douglas.
Description: Athens : The University of Georgia Press, 2019. | Includes
bibliographical references and index.
Identifiers: LCCN 2018049577| ISBN 9780820355092 (hardcover : alk. paper) |
ISBN 9780820355108 (ebook)
Subjects: LCSH: Du Bois, W. E. B. (William Edward Burghardt), 1868–1963—
Political and social views. | Capitalism—Social aspects—United States. |
Capitalism—Moral and ethical aspects—United States. | Competition—Social
aspects—United States. | Competition—Moral and ethical aspects—United
States. | African Americans—Education (Higher) | African Americans—
Economic conditions. | Racism—Economic aspects—United States. | United
States—Race relations—Economic aspects.
Classification: LCC E185.97.D73 D68 2019 | DDC 323.092 [B] —dc23
LC record available at https://lccn.loc.gov/2018049577

CONTENTS

ACKNOWLEDGMENTS

When I began teaching at Morehouse College in 2011, I had only a vague sense that W. E. B. Du Bois had published some of his most significant texts while working from an office just a short cross-campus walk from my own. Perhaps it is fitting that by the end of my first year in Atlanta, some of those very texts—*The Souls of Black Folk, Black Reconstruction in America, Dusk of Dawn*, books written during Du Bois's tenure at the former Atlanta University—would become centerpieces of my political theory course offerings. I had always thought of Du Bois as an incisive political theorist, a foremost critic of Western liberalism. But in those first few years at Morehouse, as a result of rich and often deeply moving discussions with students, I was made to see that there was more to the story and that more had to be said. It was primarily my students who led me to see that the lens of competition, the conceptual framework that I have come to refer to as the competitive society, could provide a new and generative way of getting at the distinctiveness and enduring salience of Du Bois's critique. Without a doubt, the reading of Du Bois put forth in this book bears the collaborative imprint of dozens of former and current Morehouse undergraduates, some of the best interlocutors I have known. I highlight in particular Jared Loggins, Marcus Lee, Da' Von Boyd, and Ryan Russell, now budding academics whom I have always thought of as colleagues.

For too long the broader U.S. academy has been a rather uncritical echo chamber of the competitive society, predisposed in various ways to the perpetuation of competitive animosities, if not the reproduction of a world torn between winners and losers. There have been and continue to be exceptional institutions and people, of course. Du Bois argued that historically Black colleges and universities, what we refer to today as the HBCUs, have always represented at least the possibility of another way. I can see what he was getting at. Every day I absorb the generosity and cooperative spirit, not to mention the vast wealth of expert knowledge, of so many of my faculty colleagues at both Morehouse and Spelman College. I am especially grateful to Preston King, Kipton Jensen, Al-Yasha Williams, Shay Welch, Sam Livingston, Matthew Platt, Levar Smith, Tobe Johnson, Cynthia Hewitt, Adrienne Jones, Oumar Ba, Vicki Crawford, Fred Knight, Monique Earl-Lewis, David Wall Rice, Barry Lee, Gregg Hall, and Garikai Campbell, some of whom have read portions of the book or had in-depth conversations with me about its subject matter, while others have simply enriched my thinking through passing conversation or just their thoughtful everyday presence on campus. I wish to thank also Cynthia Neal Spence, Ada Jackson, Lauren Eldridge, Gabrielle Samuel-O'Brien, Armando Bengochea, and the entire UNCF/Mellon-Mays Undergraduate Fellowship family. The annual UNCF/MMUF conference, held in Atlanta each fall, has been the most enriching conference experience of my academic career, without which this book, especially chapter 4, likely would not have been written. Beyond my HBCU communities, some exceptional colleagues have lent this project insight and encouragement. I highlight in particular Lawrie Balfour, Melvin Rogers, Neil Roberts, Chip Turner, Joy James, Desmond Jagmohan, Lida Maxwell, Robyn Spencer, Saladin Ambar, Greta Snyder, and Justin Rose, to whom I dedicate the concluding chapter. In 2016–2017, I was the fortunate recipient of a sabbatical-year fellowship at the Whitney Humanities Center at Yale University, and for their support I thank Gary Tomlinson, Mark Bauer, Jacqueline Goldsby, Paul North, and the Andrew W. Mellon Foundation.

It has been an honor and pleasure to work with the University of Georgia Press, my hometown publisher. I am grateful to Walter Biggins, who showed early and consistent enthusiasm for the project, and to Beth Snead, Jon Davies, David Des Jardines, and Elaine Durham Otto, each of whom provided skillful guidance throughout the production process. Various pieces of the book's argument, spread out over several chapters, were published in an earlier article, "W. E. B. Du Bois and the Critique of the Competitive Society," *Du Bois Review* 12, no. 1 (Spring 2015): 25–40. I thank Cambridge University Press for permission to reprint this material. My thinking has benefited greatly from the suggestions of several anonymous readers, at both the *Du Bois Review* and the University of Georgia Press.

In the end, my most heartfelt thanks go to Marcie Dickson and our daughters, Juliana and Genevieve, the three of whom have contributed to this project in immeasurable ways and have made the sleepless nights all worthwhile. To them, I dedicate this book.

W. E. B. Du Bois and the
Critique of the Competitive Society

CHAPTER 1

A More Perfect Union

> Competition, therefore, is a law of nature. Nature is entirely neutral;
> she submits to him who most energetically and resolutely assails
> her. She grants her rewards to the fittest, therefore, without regard
> to other considerations of any kind. If, then, there be liberty, men
> get from her just in proportion to their works, and their having and
> enjoying are just in proportion to their being and doing. Such is the
> system of nature.
>
> WILLIAM GRAHAM SUMNER, "THE CHALLENGE OF FACTS" (1914)

> But, bless your soul, man, we can't all always attain the heights, much
> less live in their rarified atmosphere. Aim at 'em—that's the point.
>
> W. E. B. DU BOIS, IN *DUSK OF DAWN* (1940), PARAPHRASING
> THE WORDS OF A FICTIVE WHITE FRIEND

Competition would seem to be an inexorable feature of the human situation. We rival, we jockey for position, we claw and scratch in efforts to get the better of one another. This is a simple but sobering observation, to be sure, and it is one that has long been a cornerstone of the liberal tradition, indeed a key part of that tradition's celebrated genius. In the words of W. E. B. Du Bois's fictive White friend, "We can't all always attain the heights." There will be winners and losers. But a good society, or at least a reasonably decent one, gives us a fighting chance, and, well, that's the point.

Of course, these epigraphic words of Du Bois's are meant to convey a degree of sarcasm. Certainly Du Bois was drawn to the liberal paradigm. His legacy could well be defined by a spirited effort to pry open the gates of opportunity, to expand the protection of individual rights and liberties, to give the abused at least something of a fighting chance. But Du Bois grew increasingly disillusioned with a political and economic philosophy that sought to facilitate competition among private parties. The worry was that competition would always guarantee loss and defeat for some, and if divisions between the successful and the rest could be cast as perfectly natural, perfectly consistent with a liberated humanity, then a freely competitive society would seem poised to remain a rather damning place for people of color and others historically subjected to the weight of competitive disadvantage.

This was a prescient concern. A half century after Du Bois's death, a more fully liberated America has become a more fiercely competitive place, a society somehow more freely torn between winners and losers. And as the worry would have it, women and men of color continue to bear the brunt of this apparently inexorable way of the world. In the absence today of any real public scrutiny of the competitive way of life, it will be worthwhile to revisit the provocations of a Du Bois engaged in old-fashioned ideology critique. The idea, we are told, is to relish in our freedom to compete, to duke it out for that "rarefied atmosphere." But, bless our souls, "we can't all always attain the heights." As Du Bois's later work indicates, *that's* a key point worth considering.

This book sets out to stimulate a more critical dialogue about how the public values and organizational structures of our liberal-capitalist society induce competitive behavior, often in ways that constrain or delimit good-faith efforts to confront racial and economic inequities. The argument draws inspiration from Du Bois's mature writings, principally those of the Depression era. While the commitment to competition has always been fundamental to the institutional and cultural workings of the economy and polity of the United States—"Ambition must be made to counteract ambition," James Madison said—the decade of the 1930s was a signal period in the consolidation of what we might call the competitive society.[1] In the throes of economic crisis, market reformers on both the left and the right effectively doubled down on a commitment to the competitive form and began to argue that the state had to take on a more active role in facilitating private competition. This economic argument fell in line with a broader political vision, a sense that structured competition could most effectively guard against monopoly power in the political domain and could potentially stave off the kind of one-party domination that fascist movements in Europe had begun to put on gruesome display.[2] What began to emerge—a circumscription of the political imagination by market rationality, an effort to apply competitive market principles to further dimensions of human interaction—can be said to prefigure what has grown into contemporary neoliberal orthodoxy. Recent historical work on what we might call the long history of neoliberalism has begun to document this.

If the decade of the 1930s was a watershed in the consolidation of the competitive society, it was also a signal moment in the maturation of Du

Bois's critical theory. By the onset of the Great Depression, Du Bois had begun to question the integrationist politics of an egalitarian liberalism. He urged Black women and men to engage in self-segregation, a kind of strategic racial separatism as a means of economic and political empowerment. This, of course, put Du Bois at odds with the program of the National Association for the Advancement of Colored People (NAACP), the civil rights organization that he had helped to found nearly a quarter century earlier. By 1934, he had formally resigned as editor of the *Crisis*, the NAACP's journal, and had resumed his professorship in Atlanta, where he took up serious study of Marxist thought, wrote some of his most significant later works, including *Black Reconstruction in America* (1935) and *Dusk of Dawn* (1940), and established his mature vision for a pan-Africanist educational and scholarly program.[3] In this moment Du Bois had become, as Michael Dawson puts it, a "disillusioned liberal," a critic who had lost hope in the American creed.[4] This is a framing trope that I work from throughout the book. I argue that Du Bois's Depression era disillusionment entails a generative suspicion of competition as the sine qua non of a broadly liberal political and economic legacy that endures well into our time.

To be sure, Du Bois's attitudes toward competition can be elusive. In *The Souls of Black Folk* (1903) and other early writings, Du Bois took issue with the social Darwinist discourse that was prevalent in much of the mainstream scholarship of the period. He challenged the abhorrent notion of a brute power struggle among competing racial groups. But this criticism tended to give way to a vision of another sort of competitive meritocracy, a survival of the morally and reasonably fittest.[5] Furthermore, his early conception of the "problem of the color-line" has been, and in many ways continues to be, taken to reflect a problematic *ceiling* of sorts, a line *qua* barrier to access or opportunity or perhaps to the freedom of a more openly competitive society. This reading of Du Bois's most famous statement contributed to the shaping of the civil rights agenda in the twentieth century, and it remains an implicit conceptual framework that contemporary critics of liberalism's racial contradictions tend to accept in one way or another.[6] But Du Bois was always suspicious of the philosophy of competitive individualism. He was always suspicious of the ways in which key spokespersons of European modernity sought to legitimize a spirit of contentiousness as a reflection of human behavior in its "state of nature." And by the time he read Marx in the 1930s, he had become deeply concerned with the ways in which these ideas about private competition and competitiveness, these "White world" ideas, had been made to support a logic of capital accumulation, ultimately a consolidated capitalist society that puts nominally free market actors into competitive relation with one another. Du Bois's challenge to the liberal paradigm was not simply an effort to document a rigged system and to expose a public culture marked historically by disingenuous appeals to the competitive form. His originality and enduring critical import are to be found in his disillusionment with the theory as such. As I argue in the chapters that follow, the Depression era Du Bois helps us to see that even fair competition reproduces loss and defeat for some, and as a structural characteristic of liberal-capitalist society, the competitive *form* breeds a divisive public *ethos* that feeds on the exploitation of racial and other ascriptive differences and is incredibly difficult to resist, even if we are persuaded to try.

Given the sheer magnitude of Du Bois's corpus and the extent to which his many readers have been invested in various aspects of his legacy, it is important to qualify the scope of this study. This is not a book about Du Bois's intellectual or political development. And it is meant to speak only indirectly to Du Bois scholarship and exegesis. The more direct aim is to press a broad readership into serious thinking about our competitive culture and the racial politics of a society set up to produce winners and losers. The contributions to be considered here are perhaps best thought of as provocations, as opposed to the rudiments of an alternative vision or a more traditional philosophical argument. To my mind, this is only befitting of Du Bois. He is an elusive figure, an author of "fugitive pieces," writings that run from conventional wisdom and at times risk losing themselves in unfamiliar territory, writings that do not necessarily contribute to a consistent or fully formulated theoretical narrative.[7] Moreover, by casting the mature Du Bois as a disillusioned liberal, I intend to capture a sense of frustration and philosophical uncertainty that I think is strangely appropriate to the contemporary moment. Finding ourselves caught rather squarely in the throes of the liberal (or now neoliberal) paradigm, compelled by force of circumstance to accommodate the competitive way of life, our contemporary situation does not seem to suggest a viable alternative, theoretical or practical. And yet, as this way of life continues to yield tragic consequences for so many, the frustration and uncertainty endure. In this moment, and at the very least, we might counsel the stirrings of a critic moved by discontent.[8]

In this opening chapter, I provide some historical context and establish some of the study's core concepts before turning to provide a detailed prospectus of the argument as it develops over the ensuing chapters. The contemporary neoliberal moment, hypercompetitive and racially divisive, is an expression of an underlying competitive form that has deep historical roots. These roots can be traced back at least to the 1930s, when Du Bois's engagement with Marx and his explicit disillusionment with core tenets of liberal theory shaped his mature critique of the competitive society. Contemporary scholars have gone to great lengths to show how things have changed since the 1930s, how older conceptual or theoretical frameworks—laissez-faire liberalism, neoclassical economics, Marxist theory—are simply ill-equipped to explain or make sense of distinctive features of the contemporary political and economic landscape. But core structural features of the competitive society endure, and the mature Du Bois offers a distinctive critical theoretical perspective that speaks quite generatively to the enduring racial politics of a political and economic tradition that, nowadays especially, most of us simply take for granted.

Neoliberal Disillusionment

The decade of the 1930s suggests itself for several reasons. Du Bois found himself grasping for conceptual resources at a moment of tremendous intellectual and political upheaval in the United States and around the world. This was a time in which liberalism, what has been called "the metacategory of Western political discourse," was experiencing several significant attempts at transfiguration. The emergence of fascist regimes in Europe had inspired an effort among many Anglophone intellectuals to renew and enlarge the liberal canon, to insist on a more wide-ranging tradition with a longer historical genesis, one that could be traced back to the Lockean commitment to individual liberty and limited government and that could be held up to the fascist threat as an expression of the true political values of Western civilization.[9] Moreover, in the midst of global economic crisis, the classical liberal principle of laissez-faire had come under scrutiny from the Keynesians and New Dealers, on the one hand, and by the early neoliberals who sought to renew or "modernize" a market-based political economy, on the other.[10] It was the early neoliberals in particular who sought to build a liberalism more fully committed to the active facilitation of private

competition. It was the early neoliberals who began to vivify the competitive way of life in ways that endure into our own time. There is no evidence
that, in the moment, Du Bois was attuned to any of these neoliberal theoretical innovations, what would become, what has become, the neoliberal
reformation of the liberal paradigm. But recent scholarship on the long history of neoliberal theory has revealed the Depression era emergence of a set
of normative commitments and the intellectual roots of an ongoing political project that the Du Bois of the 1930s, at least in some ways, could have
anticipated. I begin with a detour of sorts, a brief commentary on historical
and theoretical context, before returning to Du Bois.

Much has been made of the neoliberal break with classical liberal theory.[11] Nowadays it is often said that neoliberalism amounts to a kind of market fundamentalism, the celebration and application of market principles
at every level, in nearly every domain of human interaction. But what the
market and marketization entail in neoliberal theory and practice cannot
be easily squared with classical liberal doctrine. Traditionally, liberal theory
held that market interactions were simply a reflection of human nature,
what Adam Smith famously referred to as the "natural propensity to truck,
barter, and exchange."[12] The political principle of laissez-faire was meant to
capture a sense that functioning markets, and the purported leveling and
coordinating effects of economic exchange, required little more than formal institutionalization, essentially the maintenance of a currency and a
minimal protection of private property rights. But into the 1930s especially,
in the throes of widespread market crisis, defenders of the liberal paradigm
began to challenge these assumptions in ways that have had a cascading
effect on the development of neoliberal rationality.

I highlight two shifts in particular. The first derives from the neoliberal
insistence that markets are to be created and not simply left to flourish on
their own. As the French economist Louis Rougier put it at the Colloque
Walter Lippmann, the 1938 conference in Paris in which the term "neoliberalism" was coined, the "liberal regime is not just the result of a spontaneous natural order as the many authors of the Natural codes declared in
the eighteenth century."[13] For the early neoliberals, to theorize about market relations was not simply to describe spontaneous human behavior. It
was, rather, to actively promote a distinctive kind of behavior. The idea was
to implement and enforce market interactions. This point leads to a second
significant shift. Markets are appealing, the early neoliberals claimed, not

because they give form to mutually beneficial exchange relationships, as classical liberals had argued, but because they foster and support a competitive mode of economic, political, and, significantly for our purposes, social relations. In his famous Collège de France lectures on the early history of the neoliberal movement, Michel Foucault put it this way: "For the neo-liberals, the most important thing about the market is not exchange, that kind of original and fictional situation imagined by eighteenth-century liberal economists. The essential thing of the market is elsewhere; it is competition."[14]

To be sure, competition has always been a part of the liberal paradigm, a key factor in the normative defense of the theory. The idea that we ought to be free to compete in various ways has always been part of the pitch, both politically and economically. But this explicit shift in the 1930s, on the part of a group of avowed neoliberal reformers, toward a driving focus on competition, on the active facilitation of competitive market relations as "the essential thing," marks the beginning of what has become a very significant development in how we tend to think about and legitimize social inequality. Building on the work of Foucault and others, William Davies has shown that "rhetorics and theories of *competition and competitiveness* have been central to neoliberal critique and technical evaluations from the 1930s onward." And as Davies points out, "To argue in favor of competition and competitiveness is necessarily to argue in favor of inequality, given that competitive activity is defined partly by the fact that it pursues an unequal outcome. From this perspective, that of neoliberal theorists themselves," he says, "inequality is something to be actively generated, represented, tested, celebrated and enforced, as a mark of a dynamic and free society."[15] Another way to capture this point would be to say that the emergence of neoliberal thinking contributes to a shift away from the classical liberal emphasis on *equality of input*—state-sponsored emphasis on a level playing field, equal protection of rights and opportunities—and toward a more open acknowledgment of *inequality of output*, winners and losers as tangible proof that society is functioning precisely as it should. We can't all always attain the heights. And as the early neoliberals would have it, *that's the point*.

The political theorist Wendy Brown has argued that in the attempt to wrestle "the market economy from the political principle of laissez-faire," the neoliberal vision set out to "activate the state on behalf of the economy, *not* to undertake economic functions or to intervene in economic *effects*,

but rather to facilitate economic competition and growth and to econo-
mize the social."[16] Again, what begins to emerge in the neoliberal reformation of the 1930s is less a descriptive theorization of market relations and
more of a political project of marketization, what Brown calls the economization of the social. As neoliberal thinking develops into the twentieth century, drawing conceptual resources from various angles—ranging
from Joseph Schumpeter's early writings on competitive entrepreneurial-
ism to the Chicago economist Gary Becker's popularization of the notion
of self-investing "human capital"—logics of competition and competitiveness become ever more deeply inscribed in our common sense, our conceptions of self and other, our goals and aspirations.[17] In the "subtle shift from
exchange to competition as the essence of the market," we are gradually
"rendered little capitals (rather than as owners, workers, and consumers)
competing with rather than exchanging with each other." And into our own
time, as this conception of market rationality becomes ever more fundamental, Brown notes, our sense of how we ought to carry ourselves and
interact with others is made to "[mirror] the mandate for contemporary
firms, countries, academic departments or journals, universities, media or
websites: entrepreneurialize, enhance competitive positioning and value,
maximize ratings or rankings."[18] Competition and competitiveness, in other
words, become wholly normalized. And though we rarely pause to reflect
on this today, surely it is worth considering that "as a norm, competition is
unlike any other." As Davies puts it, "The most important rule of any competition is that the contestants may not cooperate or seek to act in an al-
truistic or moral fashion. It is an injunction to ignore all moral injunctions
and to act combatively in pursuit of inequality."[19]

    Throughout the book, I elaborate on these and other features of what I
call the competitive society. My point in calling attention to early neoliberal
efforts to reform the liberal paradigm, my point in highlighting specifically
the Depression era origins of what has become, some eighty years on, an
increasingly full-throated shift toward competition as "the essential thing,"
is to close the gap, as it were, between Du Bois's moment and ours. Again,
there is no evidence that Du Bois was engaged in academic debates about
the self-understanding of the liberal paradigm. He only began consciously
to refer to liberalism as such in the 1930s, and the object of his concern,
the conceptual focus of his growing disillusionment, bears distinctively
Lockean markers. But while Du Bois trucks in the terms of classical liber-

alism, while he refers occasionally to a philosophy of laissez-faire, he was never convinced that market relations were "natural," nor did he think that competition and competitiveness, and the inequalities that they necessarily reproduce, were anything but essential components of the "metacategory of Western political discourse." What is most telling for our purposes is that Du Bois was clearly attuned to the ways in which the competitive form, what has become the structural basis of contemporary neoliberal theory and practice, could be made to sustain the racial order in the United States, if not also worldwide. During Du Bois's lifetime, the Black freedom struggle had made egalitarian inroads. Black women and men had fought to be recognized as citizens with rights worthy of protection and respect. And liberalism had begun to fight back, as Du Bois knew that it would. What has emerged since Du Bois's time is a neoliberal orthodoxy replete with a purportedly color-blind celebration of competitive individualism. Wittingly or not, Du Bois anticipated so much of this. It has been said that in the move from classical liberal doctrine to the current neoliberal worldview, "Inclusion [has] invert[ed] into competition, equality into inequality, freedom into deregulated marketplaces, and popular sovereignty is nowhere to be found."[20] It is hard to imagine that a mature Du Bois could have seen anything else in the making.

Readers of the later Du Bois have begun to explore how his engagement with the liberal reformation of the 1930s can be generative for our thinking about racial politics in the age of neoliberalism. Nikhil Pal Singh has given us a rich account of Du Bois's "contribution to the wider revisions of liberal, democratic (and Marxist) thought underway throughout the North Atlantic intellectual milieu in the 1930s." Singh's analysis reinforces the reading that by the end of the decade Du Bois had grown thoroughly disillusioned with even New Deal liberalism, which, as Singh points out, had done very little to transform race relations or to challenge the underlying "herrenvolk republicanism" that had long burdened American political discourse and practice. He notes that Du Bois "anticipated (correctly) that race and race relations would be the terrain on which a wider array of social and political conflicts were mediated, interpreted, resolved, and displaced."[21] Eric Porter has argued that by the onset of the Second World War, Du Bois found himself standing face to face with the nation's "first postracial moment." This was a time, Porter says, in which a concerted scientific effort finally to debunk long-standing claims about biological bases of racial difference was being made to support and legitimize the putatively race-neutral terms of an evolving liberal discourse. And yet, at the very "moment when the falsity of race was made public, its persistence and complexity became more apparent."[22] Porter argues that Du Bois's "midcentury" reflections on precisely this contradiction can help us to work through its endurance into the neoliberal present. My work builds on these observations. I argue that in order more fully to appreciate Du Bois's enduring contributions to our thinking about racial divisiveness and inequity in the age of neoliberalism, we need to focus more squarely on Du Bois's account of how we are drawn into a web of competitive relations.

Racial Capitalism

Surely the inducement of competitive behavior has much to do with capitalism. It has been said that "neoliberalism is the rationality through which capitalism finally swallows humanity—not only with its machinery of compulsory commodification and profit-driven expansion, but by its form of valuation."[23] Finding ourselves subjected to a thoroughgoing economization of the social, most of us wise up fairly quickly to the fact that more and more aspects of our lives derive their recognized value from whatever competitive positioning we can muster. Usually we are keen to monetize our involvement in struggles for competitive advantage, but not always. Sometimes we are content simply to apply to the most highly ranked schools, to buy replica jerseys of the top-rated athletes, to accumulate the most "likes" on social media, and to let others—most certainly the investors and managers marketing those schools, athletes, and social media enterprises—find ways to turn a cash profit from our participation in the competitive society. In any case, now more than ever we tend to adopt the role of the capitalist, of the entrepreneur, of *homo economicus*, and, as David Harvey notes, "avarice, greed, and the predilections of the miser find scope for expression in such context." But, Harvey says, "Capitalism is not founded on such character traits—competition imposes them willy-nilly on the unfortunate participants."[24] This latter point is key to an understanding of Du Bois's critique of the competitive society.

Of course Du Bois had always been critical of capitalism, broadly understood. His hostility became more expansive after World War I, and in 1933–1934, when he resigned as editor of the *Crisis* and returned to academia, he set out to undertake a more careful study of Marxist thought. This I document in greater detail in chapter 3. For now, I want simply to emphasize that part of what has been neglected in the scholarship on Du Bois's complicated engagement with Marxist theory and practice in the 1930s is precisely his critique of capitalism, his theoretical critique of the logic of capital accumulation and the ways in which capitalism's value-form puts and holds each of us into competitive relation with one another. This very basic, structural feature of the capitalist form endures into our time in ways that Du Bois seems to have anticipated and in ways that give a Marxist theoretical apparatus, including Du Bois's distinctively racialist variation on it, far more staying power than many contemporary neoliberal theorists are keen to acknowledge.

One scholar who has heeded certain aspects of Du Bois's theorization of capitalism is the late Cedric Robinson, and my reading of Du Bois is indebted to Robinson's notion of "racial capitalism." In his seminal study of the Black radical tradition, Robinson argued that "the development, organization, and expansion of capitalist society pursued essentially racial directions, so too did social ideology," that "as a material force . . . it could be expected that racialism would inevitably permeate the social structures emergent from capitalism." Robinson used the term "racial capitalism" "to refer to this development and to the subsequent structure as a historical agency."[25] The idea, as Jodi Melamed puts it, is that "capital can only be capital when it is accumulating," that "it only accumulates by producing and moving through relations of severe inequality among human groups," that "accumulation requires loss, disposability, and the unequal differentiation of human value, and racism enshrines the inequalities that capitalism requires."[26] This is not a claim about the "capitalist 'origins' of race and racism," as Singh reminds us. The idea, rather, is that "racial differentiation is intrinsic to processes of capitalist value-creation and speculation," and such differentiation has the resounding effect of "changing an idealized game of merit and chance into a stacked deck."[27]

Throughout the book, I indicate several ways in which Du Bois's work prefigures contemporary theorization of racial capitalism. Du Bois indicates, in effect, that practices of capital accumulation are the manifestation of European civilization, what he might have described as a "White world" set in motion. For Du Bois, and to Harvey's point, there is nothing natural or universal about the competitive ethos. It is a reflection of a particular economic form, brought onto the historical scene by and for a particular subset of the human population. And as with the purported universality of liberal ideology, part of capitalism's staying power derives from the outward appearance that there is nothing necessarily racist about the underlying economic form. Capitalism simply acts as a kind of incubator for competitive relations. And yet racial ascriptions have been central to what Robinson calls the "inventory"—what Singh has identified more forcefully as the "permanent reserve"—of tools or resources available to those embedded in this web of competitive relations.[28] The mature Du Bois worries that the racial politics of this will continue and that the form as such effectively demands its sustenance.

One of my objectives in this introductory chapter is to close the gap between Du Bois's moment and ours, at least insofar as it relates to our thinking about the competitive society, and I want to identify two ways in which Du Bois's mobilization of a Marxist theoretical apparatus transcends contemporary concerns about the explanatory power of a 1930s critique. One concern has to do with the status of labor as a conceptual category. And in the context of a reading of Du Bois, this becomes a twofold, perhaps threefold, concern. On the one hand, Du Bois is known for his effort to vivify Black labor. Perhaps nowhere is this effort more evident than in *Black Reconstruction*, Du Bois's 1935 revisionist history of the post–Civil War period, which fashions the onset of the war in the terms of a "General Strike" and develops a powerful argument about the self-emancipation of the Black worker.[29] On the other hand, reception of Du Bois's legacy on economic matters is often affixed to his peculiar insistence on consumption, not production. Beginning in the late 1910s and carrying into the early 1940s, Du Bois argued that much of the revolutionary potential of Black women and men was harnessed in their power as consumers, in their ability to build and sustain consumer cooperatives.[30] Whereas some would argue that this latter position appears to run far afield of the traditional Marxist emphasis on the exploitation of labor and the extraction of surplus value at the point of production, others might find affinities with a broader reading of Marx's account of circulation and distribution, the expropriative relationship between buyers and sellers, not to mention more recent scholarly efforts to push Marxist theory toward an "expanded" critique of "capitalist society," including analysis of the racial and other background conditions that sustain it.[31] Certainly Du Bois was his own thinker and one for whom Marxist conceptual resources were but conceptual resources. And while my emphasis on Du Bois as a critic of racial capitalism leans toward a more expansive reading of Marx, I emphasize that my analysis of Du Bois's appropriation of Marxist theory is targeted and requires qualification. Without discounting the tremendous importance of conceptual and theoretical work on labor politics and the labor movement, I stress that my focus has to do with Du Bois's critical theoretical analysis of the ways in which capitalism's accumulative logic puts and holds each of us in competitive relation with one another.

This is consistent with how we might work through a related concern about the status of labor as a conceptual category (and perhaps also the status of consumption as a conceptual category). I have already highlighted some of the ways in which today's critics of neoliberalism are keen to dismiss the explanatory power of classical liberal theory, and this proclivity extends into ideas about labor that have been central to both classical liberal theory and the Marxist critique of it. The worry is that in the neoliberal age, long-standing ideas about labor and production have been rendered passé by the ascendency of a new rationality, a new "governmentality" in which notions of human capital and entrepreneurship predominate. "When competition becomes the market's root principle," Brown notes, "all market actors are rendered as capitals, rather than as producers, sellers, workers, clients, or consumers." And "as capitals, every subject is rendered as entrepreneurial, no matter how small, impoverished, or without resources, and every aspect of human existence is produced as an entrepreneurial one." This "transformation of labor into human capital and of workers into entrepreneurs competing with other entrepreneurs obviously obscures the visibility and iterability of class to an even greater degree than classical liberalism does," and it "also eliminates the basis for alienation and exploitation as Marx conceived them."[32] Certainly Du Bois's economic imaginary was shaped by a driving attentiveness to histories of African enslavement and the exploitation of Black labor. Certainly his thinking was shaped, scarred we might say, by attentiveness to the racial violence and dispossession that Marx once described as "capital's original sin" and that Du Bois would read into the accumulative practices of capitalism's more mature iterations.[33] And certainly the tropes of servitude and slavery haunt Du Bois's thinking about the social forms that emerge within capitalist societies. As such, we are left to wonder about how this Du Boisian economic imaginary might be said to apply today in the throes of a distinctively neoliberal order.

   In a notable study of distinctive attributes of neoliberal labor regimes, the historian Geoff Eley has shown that, "on the one hand, there are strong grounds for seeing servitude and slavery as the social forms of labor that were foundational to the capitalist modernity forged during the eighteenth century; and on the other hand, there is equally compelling evidence since the late twentieth century of the shaping of a new and radically stripped-down version of the labor contract." He notes that "these new forms of the exploitation of labor have been accumulating around the growing preva-lence of minimum-wage, dequalified and deskilled, disorganized and de-regulated, semi-legal and migrant labor markets, in which workers are sys-temically stripped of most forms of security and organized protections." This new precariousness, he says, is precisely "what is characteristic for the circulation of labor power in the globalized and post-Fordist economies of the late capitalist world, and *this* is where we should begin the task of spec-ifying the distinctiveness of the present."[34] But Eley goes on to argue that de-spite the vast differences between "today's 'deskilled' or 'reproletarianized' laborers and eighteenth-century servants and slaves," underlying processes of accumulation endure. What would appear to be "extremely varied labor regimes" in effect "sustain those processes, including those based on coer-cion." The idea is that neoliberalism reflects the continuation or maturation of an accumulative logic. "As an economic theory," Eley says, "neoliberalism specifically enshrines capital as the sovereign force in the organizing of so-ciety," and "the sole agencies neoliberalism recognizes for the purposes of the polity are the property-owning individual or corporation who are 'free' to engage in a competitive quest for improvement and the market which is the regulator of that quest."[35] Part of what I read into Du Bois's work of the 1930s is a conceptual apparatus that can help to grasp capital as that sov-ereign force, organizing and facilitating the competitive interplay among market actors and reproducing racially marked cycles of loss and defeat. And insofar as these phenomena endure into the neoliberal present, Du Bois's analysis, bolstered by comparison with Marxist critical theory, re-tains a significant degree of explanatory power.

   My qualified reading of Du Bois *qua* theorist of capital as that sovereign force also has the effect of dismissing potential concerns about changes to property ownership models in the twenty-first century. Philip Mirowski has noted that "property is no longer rooted in labor, as in the Lockean tradition." He points out that today "property rights can be readily reengineered and changed to achieve specifically *political* objectives," and he cites the examples of intellectual property, ownership claims over financial trading algorithms, and the commodification of markets themselves, each of which has been used politically to leverage the competitive positioning of their respective owners.[36] Mirowski is right to point out that property is not rooted in labor, that wealth today is not the fruit of an honest day's work, that the onset of the neoliberal order requires a rethinking of traditional concepts of property ownership and property rights claims. But the classical myth of the self-made man, what Du Bois refers to in *Black Reconstruction* as the "American Assumption," continues to play a powerful ideological role in our society. Moreover, the institution of private property ownership and the general discourse surrounding our legitimate or even natural or inalienable right to what belongs to us and not to others remain perhaps the principal institutional and discursive mechanism through which society's winners declare victory over the losers. When Du Bois begins explicitly to reference the liberal paradigm in the 1930s, he takes aim at Locke and the property question, at the liberal emphasis on private ownership claims and the ways in which liberal discourse legitimizes and naturalizes the very inequities that competitive interactions yield.[37]

Du Bois paints in broad strokes. His concerns about liberal ideology and the logics of capital accumulation speak to basic features of the competitive society, features that course through post-Fordist and neoliberal turns. The move toward entrepreneurship, toward a sense that individual actors ought to think of themselves as little bits of self-investing human capital, means that an ethic of competitiveness governs not only traditional firms but also, increasingly, individual human beings in their daily interactions with those around them. I wager that the neoliberal turn signals an expanded or more sophisticated application of the competitive form. We are today a more competitive society. We are, as it were, a more perfect union, more fully committed to a competitive form that has perhaps always undergirded the American sense of what freedom and prosperity entail. This competitive circumscription of basic ideas about freedom and opportunity, and the paradoxical way in which this more perfect union simultaneously unites and divides, is precisely what a disillusioned Du Bois can help us to reckon with.

Prospectus

In chapter 2, "Black Radicalism as Liberal Disillusionment," I argue that Du Bois identifies liberal thinking, and especially the idea that public life ought to be set up to facilitate private competition, as the defining ideology of European modernity, essentially the civilizational contribution of what he calls the "White world." This amounts to a starting premise for the broader study, and my hope is that many readers, those who are at least vaguely familiar with Du Bois, will be prepared to consider this initial claim, insofar as rudiments of Du Bois's mature position can be found in some of his earliest and best-known works and insofar as recent scholarship on Du Bois and the "race concept" has begun to expose some of the ways in which the later Du Bois comes to think politically about the "worlds of race."

In "The Conservation of the Races" (1897), Du Bois established his lifelong commitment to the idea that different race groups are organized politically around distinctive "ideals of life." He argued that what race has come to mean in the modern world has to do largely with ongoing political struggles to express or realize these ideals and to build a reality in their image. This argument finds expression in some of Du Bois's best-known works, including *The Souls of Black Folk*, where he describes his famous concept of "double-consciousness" in terms of "two worlds, two warring ideals" that tug at the identity of Black women and men in the United States.[38] And though, as recent scholarship has shown, Du Bois would go on to revise certain technical aspects of his early concept of race, though he gradually moved away from a latent nineteenth-century biologism, away from a "scientific" account of race, and toward a more sociohistorical account, he never relinquished the distinctive and foundational notion that race has been and will continue to be politically productive, that what matters politically are the ideals or values or commitments that racial communities can be said to stand for or against.[39]

Joel Olson has provided perhaps the most vivid account of how "Du Bois's mature theory of race" undergirds a Black radical or oppositional politics, one that "implies not just the end of racial discrimination but also the abolition of the white world." Such "white world abolitionists," Olson says, are the proper "heirs of a Du Boisian conception of race, one which calls for the unity of the dark world rather than color blindness, which contemplates the dissolution of the white world rather than multiculturalism, and which augurs not the fulfillment of liberal democracy but a challenge to it."[40] On Olson's account, "The heart of the white world is empire, exploitation, and privilege," a principled hostility, we might say, toward democratic inclusivity. While my argument builds explicitly on Olson's reading, I argue that in order to more fully appreciate Du Bois's contributions to our understanding of the staying power of racial inequalities and inequities today, in order to foment more robust concern about the endurance of racially marked cycles of loss and defeat in our neoliberal moment, we need a more sophisticated account of how liberal ideals and practices sustain the White world. Part of what I set out to do in chapter 2 is to show—or to begin to show, as this argument accumulates layers of complexity—that for the mature Du Bois the White world is marked by its commitment to the competitive form and that a Black radical politics requires a sustained critical theory of the competitive society.

I also begin to show how Du Bois's Depression era sympathies with Marxist methodology affect his disillusionment with liberal thinking. It has been said that Du Bois's "mature conception of race was brought on by his conversion to Marxism in the early 1930s as well as by his growing disillusionment with the philosophy and strategy of the NAACP," that his turn to Marx led him to commit more fully to the idea that race serves a partisan or propagandistic function.[41] As he put it in *Dusk of Dawn*, he came to see that racism was not simply a matter of "ignorance and deliberate ill-will," that "hidden and partially concealed causes of race hate" could not be overcome through reasoned or scientific advance alone and that these had to be fought politically by way of counterpropaganda.[42] This is an important development in Du Bois's radicalization as a political thinker, to be sure. But equally important is Du Bois's sense, perhaps emboldened by his encounter with Marxism, that liberal ideas obscure our perception of reality and our sense of what is at stake politically, our sense of, as Raymond Geuss puts it, "who does what to whom for whose benefit."[43] I argue that Du Bois's disillusionment with liberal thinking entails a variation on the Marxist suspicion of the ways in which seemingly universal ideas about freedom, opportunity, and fairness obscure social relations that benefit some more than others. In a recent commentary on Black radicalism in the age of neoliberalism, Michael Dawson reminds us that "ideological machinations are needed to encourage political quietude among the most disadvantaged by this society over and above the structurally imposed constraints of bad times. Pushed hard enough," he says, "people tend to push back." And he notes that it "is easier to avoid that situation if people believe that either their desperate situation is their own fault or, even if the system is to blame, there is no viable political recourse."[44] A critique of liberal or neoliberal ideology today has to entail an effort to unsettle what appears settled, to historicize and politicize sets of beliefs and practices that appear to be ahistorical and nonnormative.[45] As Dawson goes on to emphasize, we must set out to liberate the radical imagination, to invigorate the legacies of what Robin D. G. Kelley has referred to as Black radical "freedom dreams."[46] And of course Du Bois engages in this kind of work. But to invoke explicitly the Marxist tradition of ideology critique is to introduce a host of complications, especially today.

To what extent, for example, can we say that neoliberal ideas about competition and competitiveness cut against the objective interests of Black people? To what extent can we level claims about false consciousness? William Davies has argued that neoliberal "theories of competition" are neither ideological nor secretive in that they "do not seek to disguise how reality is actually constituted or to distract people from their objective conditions."[47] Part of the effect of the formal opening of the competitive society, what amounts perhaps to a cruel irony of twentieth-century civil rights advances, is that the competitive society plays to everyone's interests. Everyone wants to win, and everyone has a chance to win. And yet to revisit our initial observation, in the competitive society not everyone wins. Anyone can win, as it were, but not everyone can win. If Du Bois's mature disillusionment with liberal thinking entails something like a critique of ideology, it would seem to align with what Bruno Latour has described as an effort to demystify "matters of concern."[48] The point is not so much to level claims about false consciousness or to expose how a ruling class circulates ideas so as to distort the perceived interests of the oppressed. It is to foment *concern* about a society that churns out winners and losers, *concern* about our endorsement of a liberal framework that guarantees unequal outcomes and that continues to bank on racial ascription as part of the inventory of resources available to participants in the competitive struggle. Certainly Du Bois sets out to historicize and politicize liberal ideology, to expose capitalism as normative and not merely natural. Clearly he worries about how liberal political and economic theory works out quite nicely for those whom we might describe as White world beneficiaries, to put it as modestly or as least conspiratorially as possible. But by framing the contribution in terms of a critique of the competitive society, we are able to locate the traction of ideology critique in its claim to matters of concern. And this is not to diminish what remains a very difficult task, given that very few today express much concern at all about widespread public commitment to competitive principles.

This account of ideology critique carries over into chapter 3, "The Ideologies of Racial Capitalism." There I set out to expose some of the neglected dimensions of Du Bois's reading and appropriation of Marx in the mid-1930s. I argue that his reading of Marx opens the door for a theoretical critique of the ways in which the logic of capital accumulation puts and holds each of us in competitive relation. Among Marxist sympathizers who are drawn to Du Bois and among many Marxist sympathizers as such, there has been a discernible tendency to take the theoretical critique of political economy for granted and to focus on political strategy.[49] In the Du Bois studies literature, this has manifested itself in various ways. Scholars have traced Du Bois's insightful and original account of the obstacles to a multiracial proletariat in the United States. Others have sought to find appropriate labels for Du Bois's vision of a positive alternative to capitalism, to document ways in which he was a "collectivist" all along or a "socialist" all along. Others have sought to show how his avowal of Marx was shaped by the worldview of the Second International and a pre-Bolshevik gradualist or Fabian account of what socialist reform efforts would or should entail. Still others have sought to make sense of Du Bois's complicated embrace of Stalinism and Maoism and his eventual commitment to the Communist Party just years before his death.[50] These are important issues in the Du Bois studies literature, to be sure. And I draw on this scholarship in various ways throughout the book. But my consideration of Du Bois's avowed interest in Marxism in the mid-1930s is qualified by an overarching focus on Du Bois's Depression era disillusionment with liberal thinking. The idea fundamentally is to consider Du Bois's role as a *diagnostic critic* of the competitive society and to elicit a set of conceptual resources that have enduring explanatory and critical traction.

In regard to his descriptive theorization of capitalism in the 1930s, certainly Du Bois found in Marx an ally to his own methodological materialism. But it is important to stress that Du Bois never counseled any sort of economic determinism. As Singh points out, "For Du Bois, the economy was less the foundation of social organization than one of its instruments."[51]

Earlier I referred to Du Bois's efforts to press aspects of Marxist thought into
the service of a broader critique of White world liberalism. For Du Bois, the
competitive incubator that is the capitalist economic form is itself a structural manifestation of the White world. Practices of capital accumulation
and the competitive logics that such practices implement and sustain are,
as Du Bois might have put it, a reflection of the White world set in motion.
In this way, as Singh points out, the economy is for Du Bois an instrument
of a racial order. And yet, part of what Du Bois documented in the 1930s in
Black Reconstruction and elsewhere, was the way in which the postbellum
"new capitalism" appeared to be trending historically away from overt racial ordering. The trend—by no means consolidated during Du Bois's lifetime, though Du Bois appears to have anticipated the trajectory—was and
is toward putatively color-blind liberal ideals, state-sanctioned market
practices and the formal transcendence of barriers to any and all opportunities to compete. The trend was and remains toward an articulation of
the neoliberal utopia. Du Bois's materialism helps to cut through discursive
narratives that mask or legitimize enduring cycles of loss and defeat. As
Eric Porter points out, "It is not merely that discourses of color blindness
and racial transcendence mask the existence of racial hierarchies." For the
mature Du Bois, "These orientations are potentially the ideological mecha-
nisms upholding white supremacy."[52]

In chapter 4, "The Black College as a Locus of Critique," in an effort both
to consider how Du Bois's rather sweeping suspicion of the competitive society might cash out in more practical terms today and to develop further
an account of the theoretical underpinnings of that suspicion, I revisit Du
Bois's writings on "Negro education," in particular his speeches and writings
on the Black college. Earlier I noted that Du Bois's mature disillusionment
with liberal thinking included an argument in favor of strategic self-segregation. Many readers look to his defense of Black consumer cooperatives as
primary evidence of this aspect of what he called his "post-1928 strategy."[53]
But after he returned to Atlanta University in 1934, and certainly by 1940–
1941, when he launched the Phylon Institute and a new journal dedicated to
a pan-Africanist research program, Du Bois looked to the Black college as
a key driver of his political agenda. In this moment he was quite consistent
in his call for Black colleges and universities, along with other indigenous
Black institutions, to "conserve" a distinctive perspective vis-à-vis the White
world, and he was quite animated in his call for such schools to facilitate the
critique of the competitive society. With sympathetic reference to romanti-

cized notions of the West African "bush school," Du Bois insisted that the Black college in America had to set out to redeem a lost sense of universality, to commit to principles and practices of public sustainability, and to affirm a distinctive identity in and through persistent exposure of the false universality of the White world. In a notable discussion of Du Bois's role in setting the agenda for what has become the field of Black studies, Nahum Dimitri Chandler has argued that Du Bois's "singularity has, quite simply, to do with his principled conceptualization of the Negro . . . as an object of thought the horizon of possibility and becoming of which would be illimitable."[54] I argue that part of the exploration of this horizon of possibility, clearly for Du Bois the province of the Black college and Black knowledge production, entails a negative critique of a White world model of possibility, a model of the competitive form that is both limited and limiting.

Today's historically Black colleges and universities find themselves working through increasingly desperate identity crises, a predicament brought on largely by intensifying hostility from the White world. Are these schools competitive? Can they produce competitive graduates? Do they prove more effective than their predominantly White counterparts at serving the labor and management needs of the competitive society? The prevailing presumption seems to be that Black colleges and universities are dying off and precisely as they should. As we move toward that more perfect union in which everyone has a chance to compete, we can and should shed the baggage of our racial history, including these *historically* Black colleges, these ghosts of segregation past. Even thoughtful defenders of HBCUs today sometimes work within this general set of assumptions, wittingly or not. Eddie Glaude, for example, argues that we need Black colleges today, but only because we are not quite there yet, because there are still not enough minority students enrolled in conventional schools.[55] The problem is framed in terms of discrimination, access, opportunity, and not the political and economic form that White world colleges and universities reflect and reinforce in their pedagogy, curricula, and scholarship. There are others today who move closer to the legacy of Du Bois's vision for the Black college as a locus of critique. In *Between the World and Me*, Ta-Nehisi Coates celebrates his alma mater, Howard University, a.k.a. "the Mecca," and by extension the Black college as an institution, as perhaps the only hope for the cultivation of a more robust Black radical opposition to an utterly inhospitable, even unlivable White world. But Coates is a rare example. I argue that Du Bois's mature vision for the Black college is as necessary today as it is unpopular. Vincent Harding once argued, invoking explicitly the legacy of Du Bois, that Black colleges and universities must not simply emulate White world institutions. "Dark copies of dying whiteness," he said, "are no longer needed."[56] In the context of a broader critique of the competitive society, it will be worthwhile to tease out some of the merits of this unconventional perspective.

Finally, in chapter 5, "Honoring Dr. Du Bois," a title I borrow from Martin Luther King Jr.'s 1968 tribute, I highlight consistencies between Du Bois's 1930s critique and the sensibilities of the later King, whom we might describe, following Dawson, as the *other* great exemplar of Black liberal disillusionment.[57] Du Bois and King help to reveal how a twentieth-century Black radical tradition develops in tension with liberal thinking, and they highlight the challenges that our liberal-capitalist society in its competitive form, poses for transformative political movements, past and present.

Du Bois and King are frequently remembered as champions of Black culture and perspective as a civilizing force in the United States, if not also on the world historical stage. But the perspective that I recover and counsel in this book lends this remembrance a different valence, one that emboldens King's abiding calls for "maladjustment" and "dissatisfaction," one that draws closer to the negative or diagnostic criticism that Fred Moten and others have ascribed to the Black radical tradition. For Moten, the "historical mission" of Black struggle is not to civilize, not to contribute to the perfection of the Western world, but rather "to uncivilize, to de-civilize." The "brutal structure was built on our backs," Moten says, "but if that was the case, it was so that when we stood up it would crumble."[58] One overarching thought that I try to drive home is that the increasingly full-throated embrace of the competitive society signals the fragility of the racial capitalist order. The more perfect union signals, paradoxically, the perfection of its weakness. In this moment, in what has been referred to as a sort of "postcapitalist interregnum," capital as that sovereign force has begun to disclose its own limits as an integrative system insofar as it has produced something "less than a society," an amalgam of "individualized individuals" who, out of fear, greed, and an elementary interest in individual survival, are driven to competition as the essential thing.[59] Both Du Bois and King implore us to think seriously about what it means to take an abolitionist stand against an irredeemable competitive society.

CHAPTER 2

Black Radicalism as Liberal Disillusionment

"But, bless your soul man . . ." In *Dusk of Dawn*, Du Bois's 1940 "autobiography of a race concept," in a discussion of characteristic features of "the white world," Du Bois staged a series of conversations between himself and various White friends, at least some of whom must have been entirely fictional and all of whom were clearly ideal-typical symbolizations. At one point, one of Du Bois's companions interjects, in a typically patronizing tone, to remind him that opportunity and competition are and must be core public values of any civilized society. "We can't all always attain the heights," this White man says, "much less live in their rarified atmosphere. Aim at 'em—that's the point."

This figure is significant, Du Bois says, "not because of his attitude toward me but rather because of his attitude toward himself." He embodies a way in which "my environing white group distorts and frustrates itself even as it strives toward Justice."[1] This White "friend" represents the most "reasonable, conscientious, and fairly intelligent White American," the progressive liberal whose commitment to the lofty ideals of the Christian social gospel, whose belief in "Peace, Good Will, the Golden Rule, Liberty, and Poverty," are tempered, balanced we might say, by a sober realism, a sense that the human world cannot be expected to bend always or even often toward justice but that we can at least give folks an opportunity, a chance to carve out decent lives for themselves. The idea, it would seem, is that if at the public level we can commit to a principle of equal opportunity, if we can commit to a practice of something like fair competition, then we can say that we are at least striving toward justice, and for that we can rest our blessed souls in good faith. And surely there is something progressive about this approach. This is not a philosophy of racial hatred. But in the commitment to White liberal principles, in the comfortable self-assurance that this is not only a practically viable but also a normatively commendable way forward, the "reasonable, conscientious, and fairly intelligent white American faces continuing paradox," Du Bois says, a "dilemma" indigenous to the philosophy of his very own White world.

What is this continuing paradox, this dilemma? What exactly is Du Bois getting at? The years prior to the publication of *Dusk of Dawn*, harrowing years of economic and geopolitical crisis worldwide, represent a signal moment of disillusionment for Du Bois, a period in which he works through a constellation of racial and economic considerations to rethink or perhaps simply reinforce long-standing suspicions of the liberal paradigm. In this moment, we might say, Du Bois worries about a normative vision of public life in which the public sphere, broadly understood, is set up to facilitate the pursuit of private interest. He worries about how this vision, what we might refer to as a barebones version of conventional liberal ideology, fosters and legitimizes a competitive way of life, a sort of public modus vivendi in which racial antagonisms, and other hostilities derived from just about any kind of ascriptive difference, are routinely leveraged in the ongoing struggle for private advantage. He doubles down on his long-standing intimation that a philosophy of self-interested individualism is indigenous to the White world, a distinctive "contribution" of what he had once described as the "Teutonic or Anglo-Saxon civilization."[2] And in this moment of economic and political uncertainty, pressed by southern sharecroppers and compelled by a new generation of Black intellectuals who were concerned to mine the economic bases of ideological consciousness, Du Bois worries that even a more perfectly egalitarian application of liberal principles is unlikely to upset White world beneficiaries of the competitive society. Here Du Bois clings to a racial appropriation of the liberal paradigm, to a claim about White world ownership of the liberal form, as part of an intensifying oppositional politics, a burgeoning Black radicalism born of liberal disillusionment.

This is a fairly complicated set of claims, which I set out to unpack in this chapter. I begin by establishing that an emphasis on Du Bois *qua* critic of liberalism is appropriate to the historical context, that the meaning of the term "liberalism" comes into focus in a certain way in the 1930s, in Du Bois's work and in broader scholarly and public discourse. In this moment, too, as recent scholarship has shown, Du Bois's thinking is influenced by an emerging radicalism among sharecroppers and a new generation of Black intellectuals, including the Howard University economist Abram Harris, whose more outspoken critique of liberalism Du Bois works both with and against.[3] A brief review of Harris's work will put us in a better position to tease out important theoretical points about Du Bois's disillusionment with liberalism and to show how, in this moment, Du Bois commits himself to a distinctive methodological outlook, one that can be said to facilitate a critique of liberal ideology as such. I then offer a brief account of what the critique of ideology entails, and I argue that, despite his Depression era emphasis on economic concerns and his materialist methodological stance, Du Bois retains his sense that Black political struggle is, or at least ought to be, moved by a concerted effort to work out racially distinctive "ideals of life." For the Du Bois of the 1930s, a Black radical politics must stake out opposition to the dominant ideals of the White world, the public values and organizational principles that reflect the particular worldview of European modernity. As liberalism begins to crystalize in this moment as the dominant public philosophy, Du Bois takes dead aim at a political and economic ideology that legitimizes and thus further entrenches a society long torn between winners and losers.

"The Older Liberalism"

Already we have begun to consider what we might call the Black radical critique of the liberal paradigm.[4] At issue, for our purposes, is a public philosophy that encourages private competition, and for critics such as Du Bois, the "freedom dream," to borrow Robin D. G. Kelley's term, does not entail simply an effort to liberate Black Americans such that they might enjoy the freedom to compete with White people.[5] By itself, such liberation would do little more than introduce Black women and men, and people of color more generally, to a playing field that is effectively rigged in favor of the White establishment, institutionally disposed to the protection of private property and the intergenerational accumulation of White wealth. As Du Bois would remark in one early essay, "Even if special legislation and organized relief intervene, freedmen always start life under an economic disadvantage which generations, perhaps centuries, cannot overcome."[6] Moreover, as insult to injury, such a conception of liberation would threaten to shift the burden of responsibility onto those same liberated women and men. Given the chance to compete—given the "right," the "opportunity"—Black women and men would be on their own, independently responsible for any failures or shortcomings that they may endure. In a peculiar and rather perverse sort of way, this model of liberation effectively liberates White Americans by absolving them of any continuing responsibility for societal inequities or any of the hardships and suffering that competitive interaction might yield.

The gist of this critique is fairly well known. I want to frame the issue in a more distinctive way. We are dealing with a set of ideas about liberation, freedom, independence, and opportunity, ideas that are tremendously appealing, that often seem *universally* appealing, but that in practical application tend to serve *particular* interests. To put the matter in these terms is to invite consideration of the ideological character of liberal thinking. And to describe a Depression era Du Bois as a *disillusioned liberal* is to train focus on a critic of ideological consciousness. Whatever a younger Du Bois might have thought of the liberal paradigm or of what the term "liberalism" would have meant to him at the turn of the twentieth century, it is evident that by the 1930s Du Bois takes issue with the normalization of what we might describe today as a kind of liberal common sense, a way of thinking that presumes both the normative appeal and practical necessity of free or independent human behavior, and that tends to deflect attention away from the biases and power implicit in historically embedded economic and social relations. In the 1930s Du Bois starts to refer to liberalism as such, and in this period the term begins to crystalize in ways that allow for a felicitous characterization of Du Bois's critique of competitive social relations vis-à-vis the liberal tradition.

I should note that in what follows my treatment of the historical context differs somewhat from the discussion put forth in the previous chapter. There, in an effort to help make the case that Du Bois's suspicions of the competitive society pull weight into our own time, I highlighted the Depression era emergence of early neoliberal theory and the establishment of explicit, center-right appeals to competitive market principles. But, again, there is no evidence to indicate that Du Bois was privy to these debates surrounding the emergence of explicitly neoliberal theory. His critical scrutiny was, of course, trained squarely on the center-left reformations to liberal thinking and to Keynesian and New Deal challenges to laissez-faire liberalism. The point is that for the Du Bois of this period, liberal reforms, whether center-right or center-left, reflect a consolidation of the competitive form.

My attraction to Michael Dawson's categorization of the "post-1930 Du Bois" as a disillusioned liberal stems, in part, from the fact that this label is appropriate to the historical context. In the 1930s Du Bois begins to refer to liberalism for the first time and as an object of critical scrutiny. Dawson has shown that a disillusioned Du Bois took issue with "a form of liberalism that celebrates the boundaries between the public and private" and that Du Bois was concerned with "the failure of the liberal state to curb private power in order to bring about equal respect for persons."[7] But Dawson, for his part, is concerned to stipulate attributes of various strands of African American political thought, including what he describes as a wide-ranging Black liberal tradition, and he marks Du Bois, both early and late, as a kind of canonical figure here, despite the fact that Du Bois does not always describe himself as a liberal or situate his ideas and positions vis-à-vis any kind of avowed liberalism. By the 1930s, however, as scholarly conceptions of liberalism begin to change throughout the Western world, as liberalism becomes a more "widely recognized category of political discourse," Du Bois begins to invoke the term in earnest, and in this moment he is clearly worried about what this term means, about what it conceals or distorts, and about its expanding currency within public discourse.

This observation about Du Bois's usage of the term resonates with recent historiographical work on liberalism. As Duncan Bell and others have shown, the 1930s mark a turning point in the self-understanding of the liberal tradition, a moment in which the term assumes more widespread import, both in and out of the academy, and in which the meaning of the term begins to look more like what we inherit today, namely, a school of thinking that celebrates natural rights and negative liberty and that traces its roots back to the philosophy of John Locke.[8] This is not necessarily what the term "liberalism" would have meant to a turn-of-the-century Du Bois, author of *The Souls of Black Folk*, or even to the more militant, Great War era author of *Darkwater*, for whom the political theoretical object of intensifying hostility was not yet any avowed liberalism, but rather the "Freedom of 18th century philosophy."[9] Bell points out that "at the turn of the twentieth century, the dominant prescriptive narrative about liberalism in the English-speaking world identified it as a product of the late eighteenth and early nineteenth centuries, part of a cluster of ideological innovations that also included socialism." But into our own time, "at the turn of the twenty-first century, the dominant narrative views it as a product of the mid-seventeenth century or earlier." In the earlier narrative, "radicals like Jeremy Bentham take center stage," but "in the latter it is almost invariably John Locke. Indeed Locke's foundational role in liberalism today is a leitmotif of political thought, promulgated by critics and adherents alike." This "Lockean narrative," Bell continues, "was consolidated in Britain and the United States between the 1930s and the 1950s, as liberalism was reconfigured as the ideological other of 'totalitarian' ideologies, left and right."[10] And in the United States this shift was evident in, for example, the influential contributions of Vernon Louis Parrington, Du Bois's classmate at Harvard and a leading progressive historian with whom Du Bois remained familiar, and George Sabine, who, in the 1951 republication of his interwar *A History of Political Theory*, would revise his earlier depiction of liberalism to describe it rather as the "social philosophy of the industrial middle-class," a philosophy "coterminous with laissez-faire capitalism."[11] Bell points out, too, that this 1930s turn toward Locke and toward an appreciation of earlier historical roots of liberal thinking has enabled scholars to raise questions about the tradition's complicity with practices of European imperialism, questions that Du Bois himself would begin to work through during and after World War I and that seem to prefigure an orientation toward what he finally began to identify in the 1930s as "the older *liberalism* among the white people."[12]

The initial observation—that Du Bois begins to refer to liberalism as such in the 1930s, at a moment when the term takes on a new and distinctive valence in scholarly and public discourse—puts us in a better position to explore distinctive features of Du Bois's disillusionment with the tradition. Many would argue, surely, that disillusionment with classical liberal thinking was widespread in the 1930s. At the onset of the Great Depression, a broadly Keynesian critique of laissez-faire economic policy and a general concern, expressed perhaps most vividly in the work of the philosopher John Dewey, that the protection of individual rights had to be coupled with a far more robust public sphere were but precursors to the emergence of a New Deal orthodoxy, and ultimately a Popular Front coalition, that very explicitly challenged the terms of a classical liberalism understood in the Lockean sense. "The 1930s," Nikhil Pal Singh notes, "was a watershed decade for the development of egalitarian alternatives to classical liberalism," the "culmination of a long age of reform in the United States, and an unparalleled effort to resolve the contradictory imperatives in modern political life between securing the freedom of market exchange and forming a large-scale community of social equals." But as Singh and others go on to point out, Du Bois harbored deep reservations that New Deal reforms and efforts to work out a more egalitarian liberalism were and would be underwritten by the persistence of a kind of "*herrenvolk* republicanism."[13] "No sense in letting Roosevelt and the 'New Deal' mislead you," Du Bois said in 1940.[14] In this moment, he was deeply concerned that racial ascriptions would continue to circumscribe even expanded state protection of liberal rights.

Readers familiar with the racial politics of this period will know that for many Black critics, including Du Bois, "the New Deal's transformation of liberalism was really more of the same." And this is usually taken to mean simply that New Deal reforms did little to challenge the hegemony of a White supremacist public sphere. But consider that "more of the same" means also that a Lockean foundation of competitive liberalism cuts through any more egalitarian application. Singh, for his part, concludes that liberal "rights were only as good as the publics that upheld them" and that "the ethical ideal of liberalism that Du Bois wanted to preserve was the possibility of democratically constituted publics, something that had been abrogated by racism."[15] Ultimately Singh argues that Du Bois worked out a vision for a transcendent public sphere, one that was necessarily informed by the lived realities of anti-Black racism in America. This latter claim is perfectly consistent with the reading that I develop in this and subsequent chapters. My reading simply urges, in ways that Singh and others do not, a sharper focus on Du Bois's diagnostic criticism of liberal theory, a more targeted consideration of how Du Bois might be said to entertain a deeper structural concern with the paradigm itself. If "the New Deal's transformation of liberalism was really more of the same," then the Du Bois of the 1930s was able to take aim at a liberalism that bears Lockean markers, that "celebrates the boundaries between the public and the private," as Dawson put it, and that gives legitimacy to a society set up to facilitate private competition. Du Bois helps us to think about how a hallmark of classical liberal theory cuts through even its more egalitarian iterations, that is, how the liberal form as such guarantees the persistence of winners and losers.

"Private Ends and Profit"

Du Bois was not alone in his worry about the racial divisiveness of "the older liberalism among the white people." Recent scholarship on Black radical thought in the 1930s, on the "radical roots of civil rights," has enriched the historical record on an emerging generation of Black scholars who were concerned with the economic bases of the race problem, at least some of whom took issue explicitly with liberal thinking. Here it will be helpful to foreground one figure in particular, the Howard University economist Abram Harris, whom Du Bois regarded as one of the "Young Turks," one of the leading figures among a new generation of Black intellectuals who sought to apply cutting-edge research methodologies to the academic study of race relations. Harris was perhaps the most ardent defender of a Marxist approach to the study of the "Negro problem." And as Du Bois himself began to wrestle with Marx, Harris would be his go-to guy, the expert to whom Du Bois would turn for a recommendation of the "four or five best books which the perfect Marxian must know."[16] It is likely no accident that the famous opening chapter of Du Bois's 1935 *Black Reconstruction* bears the same title as Harris's 1931 book, *The Black Worker*, a text that would prefigure Harris's critique of the NAACP and that Du Bois would roundly praise in a review in the *Nation*. Let us consider Harris's 1934 report on "The Future Plan and Program of the NAACP." As Du Bois wrote to Harris in 1931, "We have got to inject into the veins of this organization some young radical blood," and "unless it is done, we are done for."[17]

In the months before and after the 1933 Amenia Conference, the now fairly well documented gathering at the summer estate of NAACP chair Joel Spingarn, Du Bois urged organization leaders to give Harris a hand in assessing the organization. That work would yield a vision statement for how the NAACP might retool and ready itself for a new chapter in the Black freedom struggle. In the report, Harris took dead aim at the organization's political-theoretical underpinnings, which he referred to as an outmoded "liberalism" that was by its nature preoccupied with the protection of individual rights. As one would expect given his Marxist leanings, Harris's driving concern had to do with the liberal emphasis on "state protection in the acquisition of property and in the employment of it for his private ends and profit."[18] For a liberalism understood according to the terms of the Lockean narrative, the property question is the cornerstone. The "preservation of property," Locke famously wrote in the *Second Treatise*, is the "great and chief end of men's uniting into commonwealths, and putting themselves under government."[19] Harris raised obvious questions about what this would mean for Black people, about how African American women and men might apply a philosophy designed initially to protect their status as chattel, then to protect what they do not have: a philosophy born and bred in the particular and exclusionary interests of White male property owners. As for the late nineteenth- and early twentieth-century application of liberal ideals in the American context, Harris pointed out that the Western frontier had, for a time anyway, opened up new vistas for property acquisition and thus had given the liberal model a "safety valve" of sorts, a way of forestalling revolutionary Black workers from realizing the limitations of an emphasis on the protection of private property. "By the 1930s, however," as the historian Jonathan Holloway points out, "the frontier had long since passed," and "property became scarce, economic rights turned into economic privilege."[20] Or, as Harris put it in his report, the "economic freedom espoused by liberalism was one that more and more became a privilege of a fortunate few."

Here I offer two theoretical points. Earlier I noted that the competitive society clings to a kind of normative realism, a sense that we cannot really escape the fact of private competition, but that a dose of reality might be made to comingle with our better ideals. The liberal emphasis on the competitive form, we might say, is meant to help refine all-too-human qualities, those nasty and brutish adversarial characteristics that cannot be disavowed. We must compete. Scarcity is real and a stern teacher. We cannot deny behaviors born of a "state of nature." Fortunately, to invoke the old proverb, "As iron sharpens iron, so one man sharpens another." Or, in the secular terms of modern liberal discourse, competition with our fellows, if subjected to the rule of law and thereby facilitated peaceably, can lead to mutual self-improvement and aggregate growth. This is what good liberals call "rising tides," ultimately a situation in which competition is rendered innocuous, if not altogether praiseworthy, because in the end everyone is better off. To be sure, the competitive society is not meant to be simply a rehashing of a Hobbesian or Lockean "state of nature," brutish and nasty as those English philosophers imagined it. The institution of government, that product of human artifice, is meant to help refine or channel natural impulses. And in the liberal tradition, the state protection of private property is a crucial mechanism for such refinement. The right to private property is a tool for individual and collective improvement, and it is one that is not in short supply. Under an egalitarian liberal government, the mechanism can be applied universally and can give every individual a weapon to fight with and a plot of land or a dollar to fight for. But while a *right* to property can be shared universally and an egalitarian liberal regime can theoretically guarantee equal protection before the law, the *lived reality* of property ownership will never transcend the fact of scarcity. Indeed, as Harris points out in his remarks on the Western frontier, in what amounts to a commentary on the racial history of the closing of the commons, the institution of private property tends toward a manufactured scarcity, a man-made division between owners and the dispossessed, a historically contingent and wholly artificial arrangement in which some have legal title and others do not. And this principled emphasis on the protection of private property effectively nurtures the conditions that require competitive behavior.

Du Bois, for his part, had begun to reflect on these questions long before he encouraged what would become Harris's scathing critique of the political-theoretical underpinnings of the NAACP. For example, in his reflections in *Darkwater* on the 1917 East St. Louis race riots, Du Bois posed the sort of question that would appear in his work with greater frequency in the decades to follow. "How far may men fight for the beginning of comfort, out beyond the horrid shadow of poverty, at the cost of starving other and what the world calls lesser men?"[21] In other words, how can we manufacture needs and wants, how can we manufacture scarcity, and thereby give ourselves reasons to compete with one another? To what extent do institutional structures and ideological frameworks incentivize and legitimize the competitive way of life? We might note, too, that implicit in Du Bois's line of questioning is a contrast between at least two visions of modern society. On one model, society is effectively set up to facilitate competition for private advantage. This is a society built for the circulation of what Harris, following Marx, might have referred to as "exchange-value." On another model, society is designed to serve human needs, "use-values." My point— the first of two theoretical points drawn from a brief look at the 1934 Harris report—is that in this moment Du Bois finds himself immersed in an intellectual environment marked by an avowed critique of liberalism, and this critique includes hard-hitting questions about what it means to live in a society committed to the principle of private property ownership and practices of competition for scarce resources.

The Harris report also raises a concern for which Du Bois is much better known, indeed a feature of the competitive society that Harris, wedded as he was to a more orthodox Marxist narrative, acknowledges but appears unwilling to accept. I highlight this point because it speaks to Du Bois's recognition of liberalism as an ideology in the classical sense. At issue is a racially charged *divide-and-rule* strategy among the industrial elite. Increasingly during the early twentieth century, as Du Bois would document in more detail in *Black Reconstruction*, industrialists were able to orchestrate cleavages between Black and White laborers, to drive a racial wedge into working-class solidarity and thereby undercut a potentially revolutionary labor movement. "As income levels and job prospects shriveled for black and white laborers, industrialists were able to play the races against each other," Holloway notes in his commentary on the Harris report. "Adding to this insult, Harris saw the National Recovery Administration's unequal wage levels for whites and blacks as 'a further extension, if not crystallization of [the] state of affairs which enables employers to divide and rule.'"[22] These concerns underscore the history of racial competition within labor. On a more theoretical plane, they speak to a political licensing of unfettered economic power, precisely what Dawson referred to as Du Bois's concern about the "failure of the liberal state to curb private power." Liberal political discourse and jurisprudence emerge here, as Marx might have put it, as a kind of legal and political superstructure, and the state appears as little more than a "committee for managing the common affairs of the whole bourgeoisie."[23] Although Harris acknowledged the ways in which Black women and men had been disserved by the perpetuation of competition among workers understood as liberal rights bearers (this, in essence, explains his dissatisfaction with the program of the NAACP), his aim was to get these ideals and policies out of the way and to get the NAACP to renounce the old liberalism, so that workers, Black and White, might finally begin to identify and act on their shared opposition to capital. For Harris, as Holloway notes, "This ideology—which when referring to whites he sometimes called democratic liberalism and when referring to blacks bourgeois fantasy—became intrinsic to the country's institutions." His thought was that "worker unity had been stymied by an economic and political ideology that supported the middle and upper classes."[24] Du Bois could accept these concerns about racial antagonism and competitiveness within the ranks of labor, but he could not—at least not yet, or perhaps not anymore—sympathize with Harris's confidence in the coming of a postracial proletariat in the United States.[25]

Harris finally gave up on his effort to radicalize the NAACP, and in 1935, when he resigned from its board of directors, he published a review of *Black Reconstruction* in which he denounced Du Bois as a "racialist whose discovery of Marxism as a critical instrument has been too recent for it to discipline his mental processes or basically to change his social philosophy," a critic who, "by temperament and habituation to the Negro equal-rights struggle," simply "cannot believe" in "a movement founded upon working-class solidarity and cutting across racial lines."[26] Indeed, as Harris himself might well have put it, Du Bois was, in this moment, a *disillusioned liberal*. But to his credit, Du Bois was able to speak to the temptations of liberal ideology in ways that Harris could not. He was able to demonstrate how practices of capital accumulation reflect a logic that puts and holds modern subjects in competitive relation, and he was able to do so in ways that Harris's "economic determinism" and persistent call for a racially transcendent proletariat simply would not allow. Du Bois's holdover racial sensibilities, his stubborn attentiveness to the "color line," as well as his subsequent insistence on what I will describe as a critique of *racial* capitalism, as opposed to something closer to a racially blind critique of capital for Harris, enabled him to see that racial and other ascriptive hierarchies have greater staying power within the disciplinary logic of the competitive society. As we move forward, Harris's more conventional radicalism will continue to provide a useful foil against which to mark and measure distinctive features of Du Bois's critique.

Old-Fashioned Ideology Critique

As the economic crisis of the 1930s wore on, Du Bois, like Harris, found himself increasingly frustrated by the public response, by the racial insouciance of the New Deal, and ultimately by what he came to regard as the misguided program of the NAACP, which he would describe in retrospect as a "most effective organization of the liberal spirit."[27] And like Harris, Du Bois came to see that any adequate explanation of the tremendous resiliency of racial divisiveness and that nagging color bar had to start with "economic motives," with a consideration of the long history of efforts to accumulate private wealth through the exploitation of Black labor. But, as he would suggest in *Dusk of Dawn*, economic motives were fundamentally interwoven with the production of ideas, and any adequate diagnosis of the problem of the twentieth century had to consider the "long history of reason" and what Du Bois would call "false rationalization."[28] Of course, overtly conservative or racist ideas would contribute to the sustenance of a racial caste system. But when Du Bois refers to "false rationalization," he seems to have in mind some of the reasons, some of the rationale, behind more explicitly progressive agendas. He seems to be concerned especially with the ways in which widely attractive ideas about freedom, opportunity, and competition could be said to disserve transformative objectives.

Du Bois had long held that the White world, that modern global movement that gave us "urges to build wealth on the backs of black slaves and colored serfs," also gave us a distinctive set of ideas, including a vision of "commercial freedom and constitutional liberty."[29] These ideas were able to take hold and flourish in the modern period at least partly because of their popular normative appeal. After all, most of us want the freedom to pursue our self-interest and to compete economically and politically. Most of us want the institutional protection of life, liberty, and estate. But these ideas are also quite convenient for the establishment and maintenance of societal divisiveness and stratification. And by the time he wrote *Dusk of Dawn*, Du Bois had begun to worry that his own project, his more or less liberal focus on "the admission of my people into the freedom of democracy," was a project based on false rationalization.[30] He came to worry that "what the white world was doing, its goals and ideals," could not be made to serve the interests of an inclusive public. The problem was not simply that "people like me and thousands of others who might have my ability and aspiration were refused permission to be part of this world." This White world was like a "rushing express," and where the apparent problem, perceived from aboard the train, had to do with the relations among its passengers, the real problem was "its rate of speed and its destination."[31]

Du Bois presents himself in this moment as a practitioner of what we might call old-fashioned ideology critique. His disillusionment with liberal thinking can be said to reflect an intriguing variation on Marx's claim that "the ideas of the ruling class are in every epoch the ruling ideas" or that "the class which is the ruling material force of society is at the same time its ruling intellectual force."[32] The thought is that widely appealing liberal ideas obscure the enduring political divisiveness of a tradition forged historically in the interests of White property owners. Du Bois began to read Marx seriously in the spring of 1933, and while he would later claim conversion to "the dictum of Karl Marx, that the economic foundation of a nation is widely decisive for its politics, its art and its culture," he never developed a theory of ideology, nor did he pursue any explicit critique of ideology in the Marxist sense.[33] And yet, in this moment of liberal disillusionment, he seems to counsel a rather strong suspicion, reminiscent of Marx's early reflections on ideology, that publicly embraced ideas and values often obscure real political divisiveness and often work to sustain an imbalance of power, in this case a racial imbalance of power. Moreover, Du Bois's suspicion of ideas and of the role that ideas might play in struggles to change the world align with a mode of critical consciousness grounded in, as he put it, the "economic foundation." Here the language of disillusionment and the intimation of being "disenchanted" or "freed from an illusion" are especially fitting.

It must be said that the critique of *ideology* presupposes a certain approach toward *ideas*, a methodological presumption of a certain *material* prefiguring. And for critics influenced by Marx, this has meant the privileging of the economic over the racial. Harris, of course, represents in this moment a more conventional Marxist materialism. His methodological approach and its effect on his thinking about race is reflected notably in his 1931 book, *The Black Worker*, where he conceives of race and racism as essentially superstructural phenomena and decries what he takes to be the abiding false consciousness of the "educated leaders of the Negro community who see only the racial aspect. Negro leadership of the past generation has put its stress on the element of race," he said in 1931. "Their people's plight they feel is the plight of a race. They turn a deaf ear to those who say that the Negro's plight is the plight of the working class in general merely aggravated by certain special features. All of the various schools of Negro thought which have had real influence on Negro life have had one end in view, the elimination of racial discrimination."[34]

Du Bois appears to have been moved by this line of criticism, at least to some extent. As Adolph Reed has argued, with characteristic attention to historical context, Du Bois's Depression era attentiveness to "the economic basis of the race problem" reflects what Du Bois might have described as a new "phase" in the development of the problem of the color line.[35] "From the turn of the twentieth century," Reed says, "at a moment when race was a paramount metaphor in social theory and political practice, it easily could appear that race would be the force most significantly shaping social relations for the foreseeable future. This diagnosis would have been all the more likely if one accepted, as Du Bois did at the time, the prevailing wisdom that assigned race such a prominent role in world history and social organization." But in the 1930s, Reed says, Du Bois "retreated from his famous color line assessment in concert with his perception of changed historical reality and his own changing interpretation of that reality. His changed perception was influenced in part by his embrace of a more Marxian view of politics, but his turn toward Marxism also reflected a shift in the discursive center of gravity away from racialist, culturalist, or other idealist understandings of the bases of hierarchy and exploitation and toward explanations rooted in political economy and class conflict." Reed goes on to point out that this trend would continue in the decades to follow, well beyond Du Bois's own scholarly work and throughout Black radical discourse and political struggle worldwide. "Explicitly racial justifications for inequality or colonial domination became less fashionable after World War II," Reed says, "and by the end of the 1970s the victories of the civil rights movement in the United States and of decolonization struggles elsewhere had begun to show clearly both that challenging the color line could succeed and, poignantly, that doing so did not resolve anywhere near as much as was implied in Du Bois's early pronouncement."[36]

I quote Reed at length to underscore the poignancy of a lesson learned through retrospective analysis of liberal idealism and hindsight observation of the limited gains of a liberal approach, however progressive in spirit. If by the 1930s Du Bois had not learned this lesson, he had at least begun to prepare himself for its core message. As Reed describes it, this lesson about the limitations of liberal antiracism, of a "color line" analysis understood to prefigure and inform an antidiscrimination politics, parallels a claim to Du Bois's disillusionment with liberal thinking. And clearly Du Bois's disillusionment was made possible by attentiveness to economic matters, by a methodological commitment to a materialism that situated Black struggle within an established economic form, one that puts and holds market actors in competitive relation and effectively guarantees unequal outcomes.

Still, despite his avowed allegiance to the "dictum of Karl Marx," despite his explicit presumption that the "economic foundation of a nation is widely decisive," Du Bois remains, as Harris aptly put it, a "racialist," a "perennial whiner over the race question," one who is not so much ill-equipped as consciously unwilling to apprehend reality through some sort of postracial lens or by the lights of a more hard-nosed economic determinism.[37] Indeed, Du Bois continues to appropriate a racial logic as part of a materialist critique of the liberal form. He comes to think of liberalism as the political and economic ideology of the White world.

"Two Worlds, Two Warring Ideals"

"To think politically," Raymond Geuss says, "is to think about agency, power, and interests, and the relations among these." It is to ask, "Who does what to whom for whose benefit?"[38] One need not trace the complicated history of Du Bois's development as a social critic to see that in the 1930s he puzzles over this sort of question and thus finds himself thinking politically about the liberal tradition. For the Du Bois of this moment, the suspicion is that ideas born of the White world bear the trace of a divisive society meant for some and not for others and that in order fully to appreciate such divisiveness, in order even to consider the ways in which our common sense might privilege particular interests, we must disillusion ourselves and explore how our ideas are interwoven with an economic form that churns out winners and losers.

At issue is the establishment and legitimation of a competitive way of life. We might think of a spirit of privatization or a driving focus on our individual pursuits vis-à-vis those around us, those whom we tend to fear as real or potential threats to our individual advancement and personal success. My sense is that Du Bois always thought of this spirit, this principled focus on individual pursuit, as a product of the White world, a characteristic contribution of what he would refer to in his earlier work as the Teutonic or Anglo-Saxon civilization. This was a civilization "built upon the 'Eternal I,'" he noted in one early satirical piece. "The 'high Episcopal Nicene creed' of the Anglo-Saxon is 'to put heel on neck of man down' . . . not that I is above Thee but that I despises Thee."[39] Du Bois suggests here that the great belief of the White world, its enduring statement of faith, is that we are individuals, and though we are not naturally higher or lower than one another, we find ourselves naturally at odds with one another. The great belief is that the nature of our worldly situation compels our self-interested behavior and that a spirit or ethic of privatization is conscripted by an inexorably competitive "state of nature." These claims about European civilizational beliefs and assumptions emerge most notably and consistently in the earlier works, but Du Bois continues to wrestle with these thoughts well into the twentieth century, certainly through the Great War and into the Great Depression. This is the moment in which the term "liberalism" works its way into Du Bois's vocabulary and very explicitly in reference to a school of thinking built upon a commitment to the individual rights bearer, to principles of individual opportunity and private competition. This is the moment in which Du Bois worries about the practical limitations of a progressive liberal emphasis on antiracism and antidiscrimination, indeed a moment when, to the irreconcilable disdain of Walter White and the NAACP integrationists, he begins to embrace segregation and a strategy of racial separatism as part of a more radically oppositional politics.[40]

"We can't all always attain the heights," but we can "aim at 'em," Du Bois's White friend says in *Dusk of Dawn*, and a most reasonable public philosophy would seem to be one that facilitates precisely this kind of private competition. Again, there would appear to be nothing inherently racist or biased about this belief. As Du Bois frames it, this perspective of the White world is perfectly consistent with a progressive liberalism that dispels the slavery and caste systems as woefully regrettable anomalies to an otherwise exceptional American way, that welcomes women and men of color into the "freedom of democracy" by protecting their right to compete as private individuals. But the worry is that this belief about an inexorably competitive state of nature is, to invoke the term once more, ideological. For Du Bois, it is not so much that we aim at the heights because "we can't all always . . . live in their rarified atmosphere." The problem is that we aim at these heights in the first place and that we lust after a detached life in that rarified air. Or rather the problem is that this competitive urge, this drive for privileged or advantaged status vis-à-vis others, vis-à-vis the other, for Du Bois the modus operandi of the White world, has been constitutive of a divisive and stratified modernity that we now all inherit. And this world, artificially constructed so magnificently that it appears only natural, compels each of us to accommodate to its competitive logic and thus to seek out ways to leverage our competitive advantage over one another, far too often through practices of racialization.

We will need to work through this claim that we find ourselves compelled to accommodate a competitive logic. For now, suffice it to say that the critique of liberal ideology builds upon Du Bois's famous, and famously controversial, account of the ideas or principles around which racial groups are said to be organized. In a recent commentary of "The Conservation of the Races," the 1897 essay in which Du Bois spells out this theory of racial idealism, Kwame Appiah notes that, at the turn of the century, Du Bois had drawn upon his exposure to German scholarship, including the legacy of Hegelian idealism, to fashion a theory that the major racial groups were collectively "striving" to realize particular ideas and that each group was essentially working out through historical struggle a distinctive sense of what it stood for as a people, as a nation, as a race. Appiah notes that, despite certain philosophical confusions, despite legitimate questions about the anthropological or sociological viability of his claims about racial groups, "what was crucial" for Du Bois's theory "were those 'ideals of life.'"[41] And while in the decades to follow, in the throes of imperialist world war and global economic crisis, Du Bois finds himself compelled to foreground material concerns. As we have seen, he retains what I would describe as a *political* theory of racial idealism, a sense that the White world is more or less committed to the application of a particular set of ideas, essentially a *liberal* political and economic vision, and that any Black politics, any Black *opposition* to the White world, would have to heed a distinctive set of oppositional ideals, an alternative set of values and principles.

Consider a telling passage from *Dusk of Dawn*, one that reflects Du Bois's take on the matter some four decades after he had first articulated the theory in the 1897 address to Alexander Crummell and members of the American Negro Academy. "It is easy to see that scientific definition of race is impossible," Du Bois said in 1940. "It is easy to prove that physical characteristics are not so inherited as to make it possible to divide the world into races; that ability is the monopoly of no known aristocracy; that the possibilities of human development cannot be circumscribed by color, nationality, or any conceivable definition of race; all this has nothing to do with the plain old fact that throughout the world today organized groups of men by monopoly of economic and physical power, legal enactment and intellectual training are limiting with determination and unflagging zeal the development of other groups; and that the concentration particularly of economic power today puts the majority of mankind into a slavery to the rest."[42] As Appiah notes in a commentary on this very passage, "Such 'definitions' as [Du Bois] offers in *Dusk of Dawn* are not, in truth, an attempt to reflect the existing reality of race; rather, they are attempts to call his own race to action." Appiah notes that "Du Bois moved on from the biology and the anthropology of the nineteenth century, but he never left its world of idealistic ethical nationalism."[43] Indeed, by the 1930s, liberal ideas, including the presumption that self-interested individualism and private competition are both necessary and attractive, are for Du Bois reflective of a White world set in motion, and while his sense of *disillusionment* is borne along by an amplification of economic logics and practices, Du Bois, ever the sentimental "racialist" according to Harris, continues to press Black women and men to work out indigenous "ideals of life," a distinctive perspective that might inform a Black radical restructuring of the White world.

Du Bois had argued in "The Conservation of the Races" that the "Negro race" had to "develop for civilization its particular message, its particular ideal, which shall help to guide the world nearer and nearer that perfection of human life for which we all long, that 'one far-off divine event.'" He noted there that "the full, complete Negro message of the whole Negro race had not yet been given to the world," that Black women and men had to "conserve" the lessons of their shared life experiences so as to cultivate a distinctive critical perspective, one that could ensure that a genuinely transcendent future, a kind of redemptive modernity, was indeed yet to come.[44] Nahum Dimitri Chandler has argued that, "above all, in this essay, and in others of the period and throughout his life, Du Bois privileged the theme of Negro *capacity*, the way in which an infinite horizon of possible forms of becoming opens within their own *existence*; a position construed such that it is radically excessive to any idea of a fixed or given essence in any simple sense."[45] Certainly Du Bois tends to veil his own sense of the substantive ideals or principles or values that might go beyond the apparently universal but actually particular ideals of White world liberalism. But he was always suspicious of a self-interested individualism that he took to be characteristic of White world modernity, and the mature articulation of this concern, vivified in the writings of the 1930s, amounts to a clear indictment of competitive liberalism as a limited and limiting political form, a false promise in the "opportunity" to pursue human capacity.

Conclusion

At issue, then, is a set of ideas about opportunity and competition, an apparently progressive vision of a world in which every individual is given a chance to live a decent life. If we can commit to a principle of equal opportunity, so the story goes, if we can commit to a practice of something like fair competition, then we can at least say that we are striving toward justice, and such a project can be said to reflect the very best of what humanity might realistically hope to accomplish. "We can't all always attain the heights," but we can "aim at 'em—that's the point."

C. L. R. James once remarked that "all political power presents itself to the world in a framework of ideas" and that "it is fatal to ignore this in any estimate of social forces in political action."[46] The Du Bois of the 1930s might have said that a liberal framework of ideas masks the enduring political power of the White world, and for women and men of color, it can indeed be fatal to ignore this. The work of the Depression era Du Bois encourages our resistance to liberal temptation. It encourages our disillusionment with a set of ideas that are, far too often, simply *illusory*, ideas that seem natural, consistent with our "state of nature," ideas that appear universally applicable, universally appealing, but that too often bear the trace of a European modernity founded and sustained on the particular interests of White property owners. By the lights of Du Bois's analysis, a sober-senses acknowledgment of this marks a first step toward serious thinking about competitive culture and the racial politics of a society set up to produce winners and losers.

Du Bois's disillusionment with liberal thinking is one component of a broader critique of the competitive society. And before turning to consider an account of racial capitalism, the other key component of the critique, I emphasize again that the overall argument is not meant to be grounded in any comprehensive reading of Du Bois's intellectual development. That said, this reading is based on an observation that the Depression era marks something of a turning point for Du Bois, not necessarily a shift toward a stronger focus on economic concerns, as many commentators have suggested, but something closer to a shift in attitude, a movement, as Dawson puts it, "from hope to despair."[47] David Levering Lewis has noted that Du Bois was always interested in political economy but that his attitude was far more optimistic at the turn of the century, when he could say confidently in a 1908 letter to the Mississippi planter Alfred Holt Stone, that "the world is starting to work for the world." Lewis points out that the earlier Du Bois exhibited a "confidence [that] he and many other liberals placed in economic and scientific progress." But, as Lewis goes on to observe, with the advantage of historical hindsight—and as Du Bois himself would see more clearly by the 1930s, confronted as he was with economic depression and the realities of global imperialism, with the aftermath of world war, with mounting evidence of the deleterious racial implications of the capitalist world system—"It was a seriously flawed hypothesis. The grim truth was that the march of science and industry tended to exacerbate race relations in the North as well as the South, rather than to improve them—at least in the short term." Furthermore, Lewis notes, "With industrialism came *competition under capitalism*, classes struggling to maintain status, and races being manipulated against one another."[48] To be sure, Du Bois's disillusionment with liberal thinking is borne along by a driving focus on the "economic basis of the Negro question." But this disillusionment reflects a distinctive critical attitude or concern, a disposition born of an utter lack of confidence in the prospects of a society committed to the competitive form.

The Ideologies of Racial Capitalism

In mid-May 1933, at a conference in Washington, D.C., on the "Economic Status of the Negro," Du Bois took dead aim at the spirit of American capitalism. "It is extraordinary," he would say, "how the patterns of the present setup of business have completely captured our imaginations." And "unless we suffer a spiritual revolution," unless we "give up the idea that the chief end of an American is to be a millionaire," unless we "envisage small incomes and limited resources and endless work for the larger goals of life, unless we have this, nothing can save civilization either for white people or black."[1] Though it remains an understudied text, the so-called Rosenwald Conference lecture provides an illuminative entrée into Du Bois's Depression era thinking about economic matters, including his sense that an ethic or spirit of competitive liberalism ought to be subjected to sharper critical scrutiny. In many ways, it represents what Du Bois would call "the beginning of a new line of thought." As he would recall later, this was the period in which he genuinely "became interested in the New Deal," when he began to "supplement the liberalism of Charles Sumner with the new economic contribution of the 20th century," and when he "began to read and study Karl Marx."[2] By 1933 Du Bois found himself at irreconcilable odds with the NAACP, and he resumed his professorship at Atlanta University, where he would offer graduate seminars on the "Economic History of the Negro" and "Karl Marx and the Negro Problem." *Capital* was the centerpiece of the reading list.[3] He found it most "inspiring," he would recall of that first semester back in Atlanta, "to be in a school again among intelligent and enthusiastic young folk," to be "reading and learning with the class."[4]

Among readers of the later Du Bois, there appears to be broad consensus, developed over several decades, that while he works around the edges of Marxist theory, while his emphasis on the self-activity of Black labor and the history of African enslavement enrich theorization of class consciousness and the "primitive accumulation" of capital, and while he is quite vocal about his embrace of "the dictum of Karl Marx, that the economic foundation of a nation is widely decisive for its politics, its art and its culture," in the end, when it comes to the underlying theoretical apparatus, Du Bois is just not a very good Marxist or is at least not very thorough.[5] Cedric Robinson, for example, has argued that Du Bois does not work from an account of "the contradiction between the modes of production and the relations of production," as Marx does, but develops instead a critique of capitalism based on nuanced documentation of "the ideologies of racism and, to a lesser extent, individualism."[6] Some years ago William Gorman argued that Du Bois's writings suggest something like what Marx would have derided as a "utopian socialism," that Du Bois lacked the "theoretical equipment" of Marxist analysis, and that he was strong on sociology and history but rather weak on economics.[7] And it was said in the mid-1930s, upon publication of a series of *Crisis* articles on Marxism and Black liberation struggles, that Du Bois's Marxism was but a "literary device," that he needed to brush up on the "theory of value," and that his economic analyses could benefit from a more serious engagement with Sidney Hook's then-groundbreaking studies of Marxist thought.[8]

This chapter will give us an opportunity to flesh out further dimensions of Du Bois's economic analysis and to push back on the insinuation that he lacks "theoretical equipment." By way of a comparative reconsideration of two foremost critics of modern capitalism, I attempt to articulate a set of theoretical resources that can help to disclose and foment concern about root sources of persistent societal divisiveness, in particular the structural basis of the competitive ethic, the competitive individualism that, in our neoliberal moment especially, holds each of us so firmly in its grip. To that end, the chapter's driving interpretive claim is fairly straightforward. For Du Bois, the postbellum consolidation of American capitalism, which he describes so vividly in *Black Reconstruction* as the tragic "counterrevolution of property," signals the imposition of a distinctive social form, one that requires a spirit of privatization and an ethic of competitive individualism, one that, given its historical genesis, feeds on the enforced exploitation of racial ascription in the desperate and endless hunt for competitive advantage.

Ultimately Du Bois gives us an account of what Robinson calls "racial capitalism," or the ways in which "the development, organization, and expansion of capitalist society pursued essentially racial directions, so too did social ideology," the ways in which racialism permeated the "social structures emergent from capitalism" and assumed a kind of "historical agency" in its own right.[9] Du Bois's thinking aligns, furthermore, with what Nancy Fraser and Michael Dawson have described more recently as an "expanded conception of capitalism," one that positions racial inequality centrally among the necessary "'background' conditions, the 'hidden abodes,' that enable" the circulation and accumulation of capital.[10] The notion of racial capitalism, which in Du Bois's work and elsewhere draws key insights from Marxist analysis but clearly moves beyond the scope of Marx's work, is richly generative for a renewed critical encounter with contemporary capitalism and its crisis tendencies, as the ongoing proliferation of scholarly interest in the concept attests.[11] And well established is Du Bois's status as a central figure in this emerging literature.[12] What I point to here, and what I think emboldens into our own time the critical disclosure of capitalism's "hidden abode of race," is how pervasive ideologies of competition and competitiveness, which are widely appealing precisely because of their postracial presentation, forestall a new abolitionism and a proper reckoning with the White world.

In pursing these claims, I underscore the category of the political and how Du Bois's work gives us an explicitly *political* theory of racial capitalism.[13] I do so in two ways. First, I argue, Du Bois's avowed Depression era interest in Marx coincides with a prioritization of *politics* over *ethics*, an emphasis not on individual responsibility but rather on a broader structural critique of the social form that regulates individual behavior and that often delimits individual capacity to resist the worst of the competitive ethos. Into our own time we continue to fantasize about the critical import of the ethical register as if a cultivated generosity or a friendlier or more virtuous disposition will somehow offset the regulative logic of a set of social relations that are reproduced through the production and circulation of capital. The Depression era Du Bois helps to expose this ethical fantasy and to underscore the need for both structural critique and, ultimately, revolutionary transformation. Du Bois's grappling with Marx and racial capitalism also underscores a prioritization of *politics* over *economics*, a rethinking of the sense, again so integral to today's neoliberal imaginary, that the "opening" of the competitive society is consistent with the liberation of human nature, with the freeing of a kind of competitive instinct, and that a formally free, what liberal apologists might call an "unregulated," economic sphere bespeaks somehow a movement beyond the kind of political control, the brute political manhandling, that accompanied African enslavement. While scholars continue to argue over the ambiguities and limitations of Marx's account of "primitive accumulation" and the transition to capitalism from what Marx called its "prehistory," Du Bois's thinking about the consolidation of modern capitalism never wavers from a kind of zero-sum realism, an abiding and deeply tragic sense in which economic gains are always already political victories, always enforced, a sense in which the competitive society is always imposed, an expression of the White world set in motion.

Before turning to the substance of the discussion, it will be helpful to offer a preemptory point of clarification about this key term of our analysis. In many of Du Bois's economic writings, references to *cooperation* greatly outnumber references to *competition*. And my sense is that many readers interested in Du Bois's economics tend to focus on his positive economic program, on specific and concrete proposals for economic transformation, which so often issue in calls to develop and strengthen consumer and producer cooperatives.[14] The parting charge of the Rosenwald lecture, for example, is a call to "give the world an example of intelligent cooperation, so that when the new industrial Commonwealth comes, we can go into it as experienced people and not again be left on the outside as mere beggars."[15] To be sure, it takes real courage to put forth positive proposals for revolutionary change, as Du Bois the scholar-activist so often did. It is much easier for subsequent generations to condemn in hindsight after specific proposals peter out, as armchair critics have done and continue to do. But Du Bois's persistent emphasis on economic cooperatives and his references to the prospects of a "planned economy" can be read as a kind of determinate negation of the anti-cooperative and outwardly unplanned ethos of American capitalism. Readers of Du Bois have been relatively quiet, if not altogether silent, on his political-economic critique of the competitive society. This chapter aims to help fill that void.

"The American Theory of Compensated Democracy"

In "Looking Forward," one of the more theoretically rich chapters in *Black Reconstruction*, Du Bois tells a story about a sort of national confusion that sets in after the Civil War, a confusion between "two quite distinct but persistently undifferentiated visions of the future." Certainly there persisted the ideals of the Abolitionists, the best or most radical of which Du Bois would read into an emerging "theory of universal democracy." But this vision "lay confused in so many individual minds" with "the development of industry in America" and with "a new industrial philosophy." Du Bois's concern is that the American democratic imaginary, the popular sense of what public life is and ought to be, had become increasingly circumscribed by a distinctive economic rationality and that this trend, this essentially ideological confusion, signals a deeply antidemocratic evacuation of American public life.

The confusion derives, Du Bois says, from the persistence of what he calls "the great American Assumption." This is clearly a variation on the idea of the "American Dream," a notion popularized four years earlier, in 1931, by the historian James Truslow Adams.[16] At work here are widely familiar American tropes, including the principle of economic opportunity, the thought that political legitimacy begins with a guarantee of "freedom from government interference with individual ventures," and the assumption—and for Du Bois this is really the foundation of it all—that "wealth is mainly the result of its owner's effort" and that "any average worker can by thrift become a capitalist."[17] Readers of *Black Reconstruction* are likely to be familiar with Du Bois's treatment of the American Assumption, which plays a prominent role at crucial points throughout the narrative. And certainly Du Bois's zero-sum realism sets out to ground the dreamy illusion that, with a little grit and determination, anyone can become a capitalist and get ahead. We will have occasion to revisit this theme later in the chapter. But it will be helpful first to scrutinize a subsidiary notion, a more specific notion, which Du Bois captures in a passing reference to "the American theory of compensated democracy." Du Bois does not really elaborate on this theory. But it is perhaps a more fecund phrase, especially when it comes to our thinking about a vision of the future born of the development of industry in America. There are at least two ways in which we might interpret the reference.

One is to read into it the more straightforward notion that, in the wake of the Civil War, as at other breaking points in the history of American democratization, elites were forced to throw a bone to the masses, to grant the lower ranks a share of the governing authority. And yet the sense from on high was always that reciprocal concessions had to be made, that democracy had to be *compensated*, and that any new political arrangement had to retain some degree of hierarchy, privilege, status, perhaps the endurance of a certain myth of a "founding" governing lineage. To be sure, to students of democratization, there is nothing particularly new or noteworthy about this sort of bargaining among elites and masses. But, for our purposes especially, it is telling that Du Bois mentions this postbellum "theory of compensated democracy" in tandem with the rise of the "philosophy of 'shirt-sleeves to shirt-sleeves,'" or the notion that, in a capitalist society, social mobility is not a smooth, one-way upward journey, that boom and bust cycles cash out at the site of lived experience, and that "a careless spendthrift though rich might become a pauper."[18] In some sense Du Bois is simply rehearsing his long-standing concern, captured memorably in *The Souls of Black Folk*, that aspiring Americans, ever stooping for mere gold, so often find that gold accursed, like the fabled Atalanta.[19] But in 1935, as a reader of Marx, Du Bois had to have been more attuned to the idea that, as history repeats itself, as waves of democratization are bought at the price of increasingly sophisticated elite bargaining schemes, the joke falls harder and harder on the masses—first time as tragedy, second, third, fourth, fifth time as bloody farce.[20] While the bargain may be sweet enough to tempt the buyer, it is ultimately nothing more than a raw deal, and we see this when we reflect a bit more deeply on this reference to an "American theory of compensated democracy."

Back of this idea, as Du Bois might put it, we find the rudiments of a broader and more revealing theory, what I might fashion rather as a theory of *compensatory* democracy. And this is a second way to interpret Du Bois's phrase, though it is perhaps only an alternative elaboration on the same point. The idea is that we come to think of public life increasingly in terms of our private investment. Democracy—our very ability to engage or interact publicly, to concern ourselves with issues that affect the many—is meaningful to us only insofar as we are able to see, or at least confidently to speculate on, some sort of tangible return on our individual investment. The sense is that we must be able to get something from public life, we must be privately *compensated*, or else it is just not worth our time and trouble. On this model, public life becomes but a tool, an artificial mechanism intended to serve private enrichment. Whether we want to call this a model of compensatory democracy, or stakeholder democracy, or just old-fashioned liberal democracy, clearly Du Bois is worried about what this way of thinking means for Black people, about how this concept of public life, this sense of what democracy is all about, is likely to fuel the desperation and divisiveness of the competitive society.

On this theme of compensation, regarding the sense that a certain compensatory logic has come to affect our thinking about the democratic experience, it will be helpful to remark briefly on Marx's account of the money fetish, which helps to open a window onto a deeper structural critique of capitalism. In abstraction, the notion of compensation—a rendering of equivalents, a balancing of the scales—would appear potentially quite consistent with the leveling, egalitarian thrust of the democratic ideal, presumably including Du Bois's vision for a more public facing "universal democracy." But in context, the sense of compensation at work in this "American theory of compensated democracy" is clearly circumscribed by the logic of capital accumulation, by the drive to acquire the so-called universal equivalent, money. This tendency is only exacerbated in our own time, in which just about any reference to "compensation" is quickly translated into a calculation of dollars and cents, a calculation of how reciprocation quite literally cashes out.

Why is this significant? In *Black Reconstruction*, in his thinking about the confusion between two visions of the American future, Du Bois finds himself reflecting on a particular moment in the consolidation of the American capitalist system, a moment in which former slaves had won for themselves the prospect of some compensation for their labor only to be confronted by a more covert brand of servitude in the commodity form, in the commodification of what had been thought to consist in extra-economic spheres of human activity. This is, of course, one of Du Bois's persistent concerns—how "the slave went free; stood a brief moment in the sun; then moved back again toward slavery," how "the concentration particularly of economic power today puts the majority of mankind into a slavery to the rest."[21] What Marx helps us to see, and Du Bois appears increasingly attuned to this, is that the commodity fetish, the money fetish, works to congeal and stabilize a model of society in which the very source of the community, the mechanism that binds together—increasingly, the exchange of money—is also, and contradictorily, the source of anticommunity, the mechanism that tears people apart. As the so-called universal equivalent, Marx says, money can be understood as "the radical leveler," that which "extinguishes all distinction." But it is "also itself a commodity, an external object capable of becoming the private property of any individual." And as such, "the social power becomes the private power of private persons." In other words, the circulation of commodities, the exchange of money, the mediated activity that renders the market a site of social coordination, is in fact a kind of contradictory "social retort," which, in unification, spits out division. Like Du Bois, Marx is concerned about a model of society in which "each looks only to his own advantage," and "the only force bringing [people] together, and putting them into relation with each other, is the selfishness, the gain, and the private interest of each." For Marx and perhaps increasingly for Du Bois, the larger concern has to do with the emergence of a commodity or money fetishism that, by its own internal dynamic, works to institutionalize this liberal model of society.[22]

Du Bois, for his part, does not explicitly tease out these finer theoretical points, and though he was seriously engaged with Marx's texts during the writing of *Black Reconstruction* and he was actively reading and discussing *Capital* with his students in Atlanta, we can only speculate on the extent to which Marx's theories directly inform his criticism of this period. And there are good reasons to resist getting involved in turf wars over whether or not to label Du Bois a "Black Marxist." Although valuable in many ways, scholarly efforts to claim or disclaim Du Bois as a representative of this or that intellectual tradition can discourage the use of multiple intellectual and methodological resources in the broader effort to theorize and confront real-world problems reminiscent of Du Bois's struggle and in this case also Marx's.[23] When Du Bois says, for example, in 1933 in the Rosenwald Conference lecture that we "are ignorant of the function and meaning of money," that "we have lied for so long about money and business that we do not know where the truth is," surely we can read into this a set of concerns about commodification, about how the drive for wealth and for compensation in the form of money obscures a deeper truth about the liberal-capitalist social form and about a conception of public life bent on the service of private interest. And here it is not unhelpful to enlist the services of Marx, as Du Bois himself claims to have done.

"The Coercive Laws of Competition"

However else he might have come down on the matter over the long course of his remarkably productive life, it is fair to say that in the 1930s Du Bois's concerns about the "lust for gold" do not reflect the apprehensions of a mild-mannered ethicist who might simply encourage his readers to resist greedy behavior. Du Bois's Depression era writings reveal a properly dialectical thinker for whom particularities are reflective of broader social totalities, a properly political thinker for whom individual ethical choices are largely circumscribed by the structural workings of established institutional form. And for Du Bois, the form is the "new capitalism," a more fully integrated world system that would prove to be more intensely competitive at every level. "Within the exploiting group of New World masters," he said of this post-Reconstruction model, "greed and jealousy became so fierce that they fought for trade and markets and materials and slaves all over the world until at last in 1914 the world flamed in war," leaving "grotesque Profits and Poverty, Plenty and Starvation, Empire and Democracy, staring at each other across World Depression."[24] Among the workers, too, greed and jealousy became so fierce that "color castes" warred against any mutual interest, effectively foreclosing in advance even the possibility of revolutionary working-class consciousness.

This is usually a point at which readers identify a significant contrast between Du Bois and Marx or perhaps between Du Bois's sober senses and the political-programmatic shortsightedness of orthodox Marxism. The latter, so the story goes, is wedded to a rather optimistic vision of the consolidation of revolutionary consciousness, a working-class consciousness that is thought to be all but destined to root out the irrationalities of racial prejudice and divisiveness. As evidenced by Du Bois's disagreements with Abram Harris, this is a vision that Du Bois, clinging perhaps to an increasingly general sense of disillusionment, simply could not abide. But whatever contrasts are to be drawn between Du Bois's tragic realism and the political naiveté of doctrinaire Marxism, it must be said again that Marx's thought—expressed in the texts that Du Bois was reading and teaching at the time—provides a set of theoretical resources with which to diagnose extant reality and to confront the ongoing miseries of capitalist society. In this effort to reconstruct and build out Du Bois's critical theory of the structure of the postbellum "new capitalism," it is again worth leaning into Marx.

As more and more human beings find themselves subject to the pull of commodification, bound together by the circulation of exchange value and money, another contradiction begins to emerge, which Marx refers to as a "contradiction between the *quantitative limitation* and the *qualitative lack of limitation* of money," a contradiction that "keeps driving the hoarder back to his Sisyphean task: accumulation." In *Capital*, this is the first mention of the drive for accumulation, and it is significant that Marx introduces this phenomenon in the context of a discussion about how a social form is constituted and sustained. Part of what Marx is concerned with is the outgrowth of a distinctive rationality, a regulative logic that maps onto capitalism's value-form, an ethic of behavior that derives from the way in which human beings are put into material relation with one another. We must keep in mind that for Marx, the reproduction of capitalist society is to be understood in its dialectical totality, as a process, the "ceaseless augmentation of value, which is achieved by the more acute capitalist by means of throwing his money again and again into circulation."[25] Marx's point is that we are driven to accumulate in a socially significant way. It is not that our participation in the production and circulation of value teases out some sort of hoarding instinct or that capitalism simply allows for a more widespread realization of an acquisitive urge that we might read into human behavior across time and place. Rather, capitalism's value-form induces an outward aggressiveness, such that the drive to accumulate, to "throw our money again and again into circulation," puts each of us into hostile relations with those around us. (And it is worth noting here in the reference to Sisyphus the insinuation that, if only we had more control over our situation, we might be able to put an end to, or at least rethink, this rather senseless behavior.)

It will be helpful to consider what Marx called the "coercive laws of competition," as Marx's formulation of this point provides a valuable way of transitioning into Du Bois's take on racial capitalism and the endurance of a zero-sum political economy. And in our own neoliberal moment, at a time in which, as Du Bois might put it, "the patterns of the present setup of business have completely captured our imaginations," surely this is a phenomenon with which we are all familiar. The idea is that we must stay on the offensive. We must grow and expand and create new markets, new innovations, new technologies. We must accumulate more capital and we must reinvest. And the explanation, the rationale, is that we *must* do this *in order to stay competitive*. For if ever we slow up, if ever we stagnate or become complacent, we risk falling behind vis-à-vis our competitors. This idea that we pursue our private interest *because* we fear competition, this notion that the practice of capital accumulation is natural *because* it is simply a kind of instinctive response to an inexorably competitive environment, is very nearly a perfect rationale for why we have "grotesque Profits and Poverty, Plenty and Starvation," a society torn between winners and losers. When we compete, as we must, there will always be losers. Such is just the nature of the beast.

But of course Du Bois encourages us to think differently about the nature of this beast. Du Bois seems to suggest, as Marx does, that a competitive ethic gets built onto a society oriented toward private capital accumulation. In the *Grundrisse*, Marx says that competition does not establish the laws of capital accumulation, "but is rather their executor," that "unlimited competition is . . . not the presupposition for the truth of economic laws, but is rather the consequence."[26] And though Marx does not elaborate on this remark, the idea seems to be that the drive for capital accumulation—that outward aggressiveness, that imperial push for more, that will-to-power essence of modern capitalism—effectively encourages private competition in such a way that competition comes to appear natural and inevitable. The idea seems to be that competition *follows from* the drive for capital accumulation and not the other way around.[27] And even to entertain this thought is to invite consideration of whether or not this competitive way of life, this ethic of privatization, is as natural and inexorable as we tend to presume.

To put this back into the terms of Du Bois's analysis, the critique is that what Du Bois refers to as the "use of capital," by which he means the widespread embrace of the capitalist mode of production, is in many ways the defining material legacy of the White world and that, as more of us assume the freedom to participate in a society oriented principally toward capital accumulation, our aggressive pursuit of private interest is less a willful expression of a necessary and universal way of life and more a defensive reaction, a tragic accommodation of a divisive logic set in motion by and for the particular interests of the White world.[28]

"The Counter-Revolution of Property"

It is important to keep in mind that Marx's critique of political economy is an academic critique of the theories and assumptions of the classical political economists, capitalism's intellectual "sycophants." For the most part, *Capital* takes up and challenges bourgeois theory on its own terms. And in many ways, Du Bois would appear to be broadly sympathetic with the *the-*

oretical critique. But Du Bois is in many ways a more practical thinker, or at least he found himself engaged in the struggle in a more practical and particular way. In his efforts to counsel the perspectives of Black women and men, Du Bois may well have revealed himself to be, as David Levering Lewis puts it, "the incomparable mediator of the wounded souls of Black people."[29] Ultimately Du Bois is concerned to show, with sober senses, that a *racialized mode of political domination*, which gets obscured in Marx in the discussion of the "primitive accumulation" of "capital's prehistory," endures into a more "liberated" society, a more consolidated capitalist economy marked by widespread commodification and compensatory relations. Du Bois sets out to disillusion his readers of the familiar tropes of endless growth and rising tides, the "American Assumption" and the idea that the "chief end of an American is to be a millionaire." His commentaries encourage readers to wallow instead in the tragedies of the zero-sum game, to acknowledge that, as we are conscripted into competitive social relations and disciplined by capitalism's regulative logic, we confront a world in which some will win and others, often those already "wounded souls," will lose. And despite all the ideological enthusiasm, despite capitalism's best sycophantic cheerleading, the White world, the beneficiaries of what Marx called the "original sin" of primitive accumulation, would have it no other way. Du Bois wants us to see this, reflect on this, and reject wholesale, as new abolitionists, the "ideals . . . of our twisted white American environment."[30]

Here there are two key points that we ought to consider. The first is that Du Bois refuses to relegate the political violence of "the so-called primitive accumulation" to capitalism's prehistory. In Marx there is a degree of ambiguity here, but clearly Du Bois reads into the "new capitalism" the straight-up political violence of the zero-sum game, the sort of brute power play in which one's gain is necessarily another's loss. And of course capitalism's "original sin" was never color-blind, which leads to a second point, namely, that capitalism's enduring sinfulness cannot be color-blind. I want to underscore the idea that as Du Bois puts it in *Darkwater*, the opening of the competitive society signals the "discovery of personal whiteness."[31]

The first point follows from an observation about how Marx comes at his subject and how his critique of capitalism tends to work from the assumptions of classical political economy. At least initially, Marx's critique concedes a degree of formal equality among those who, as the bourgeois theorists would have it, are said to pursue mutual benefit through market exchange. Marx explores whether or not a certain level of reciprocity, a certain give and take among supposedly free and equal subjects, could even in theory lift waters and boats. Of course, Marx goes on to challenge the conclusions of the bourgeois economists by arguing that the systemic exploitation of labor-power, combined with a superstructural commitment to the institution of private property, leads not to mutual benefit but rather to intensifying stratification, wealth accumulation at one pole and widespread pauperization at the other. The point is just that on a conceptual level, Marx's theory of capitalism, like that of the classical political economists, requires the commodification of labor-power, the ability of the worker to sell her labor-power in exchange for a wage. By the terms of the academic debate, as a matter of strict categorical precision, any other mode of production, including a system based on the exploitation of slave labor, is relegated to prehistory.

Of course, Marx does address the transition to wage labor and market exchange, the "so-called primitive accumulation" of capital, and here he simply has to move beyond the assumptions of the classical political economists. Here no stretch of the historical imagination, not even the fabrications of capitalism's most skilled sycophants, could lead one to retain any presupposition of equal standing among interacting subjects. For in the process of transforming the producer into a wage laborer, of turning labor-power into a commodity, in the process of "divorcing the producer from the means of production" and establishing the conditions for the "capital-relation," we confront the "notorious fact that conquest, enslavement, robbery, murder, in short, force, play the greatest part."[32] Indeed Marx's account of primitive accumulation lays bare the zero-sum brutality of capitalism's prehistory, the ways in which earlier manifestations of social control have tended to exhibit more naked political manhandling.[33] Surely this is a more adequate conceptual inroad for thinking about how, for example, the racial order of the antebellum American South, indeed of the so-called New World, was brought together and enforced. But again, in the context of the broader critique, Marx's discussion of primitive accumulation is exceptional. The broader critique is intended to flesh out the workings of mature capitalism, to show how, as commodification and compensatory relations become more widespread, the noisy political relations of capitalism's prehistory are supplanted by the "silent compulsion of economic relations."[34]

Though Marx was not deaf to the racialism of the "original sin," his theory of capitalism obscures the endurance into capitalism's organizational form of a racialized mode of political domination.[35]

Du Bois, for his part, is never compelled to accept bourgeois political economy on its own terms or to generate an academic teardown of mainstream economic theory. His economic commentaries set out from the real world of capitalism's miseries, the lived histories and ongoing experiences of the Black worker, whom he describes famously as "the foundation stone not only of the Southern social structure, but of Northern manufacture and commerce, of buying and selling, of the English factory system, of European commerce, of buying and selling on a world-wide scale."[36] Du Bois may set out to build on Marx's account of primitive accumulation and to highlight the violent historical bases of capitalist modernity, the ways in which Europe's "urges to build wealth on the backs of black slaves and colored serfs" manifested themselves in unspeakable brutality. But he is far more attuned to the ways in which the politics of capitalism's prehistory, the mode of political domination used to found and retain the "color bar," come to accompany mature capitalism's organizational form. He comes to see that "the color bar could not be broken by a series of brilliant, immediate assaults," that behind those "urges to build wealth on the backs of black slaves and colored serfs . . . followed those unconscious acts and irrational reactions, unpierced by reason, whose current form depended on the long history of reason, whose current form depended on the long history of relation and contact between thought and idea."[37] The point is that, beyond any affinities with Marxist theory, Du Bois's critique of capitalism requires a distinctive conceptual supplementation, for what we get ultimately is a critique of *racial* capitalism.

If slavery is capitalism's "original sin," then, as Du Bois puts it in *The World and Africa*, a secondary "sin of capitalism is secrecy: the deliberate concealing of the character, methods, and results of efforts to satisfy human wants."[38] For Marx, this secrecy obscures the exploitation of labor-power at the point of production; as Nancy Fraser reminds us, "Marx looked behind the sphere of exchange, into the 'hidden abode' of production, in order to discover capitalism's secrets." This move, surely, has proven to be immensely revelatory in Marx's day and well into our own. But, as Fraser goes on to argue, in order to develop "conceptions of capitalism and capitalist crisis that are adequate to our time," we need to "seek production's conditions for possibility behind that sphere, in realms still more hidden."[39] And as Michael Dawson has argued, a necessary background condition that enables the production and circulation of value in capitalist society is precisely the "'hidden abode of race': the ontological distinction between superior and inferior humans—codified as race—that was necessary for slavery, colonialism, the theft of lands in the Americas, and genocide" and that "produced and *continues to produce* the boundary struggles" characteristic of capitalist expropriation.[40]

Earlier I said that the theory of racial capitalism, which Jodi Melamed has fittingly described as an "activist hermeneutic," continues to inspire and shape richly generative thinking about what a critical theory of capitalism relevant to our time requires. The more targeted point worth considering here is what a recovery of the "hidden abode of race" says about the unhidden, perhaps deliberately unhidden, popular commitment to competition and competitiveness. Melamed has argued that "we need a more apposite language and a better way to think about capital as a system of expropriating violence on collective life itself" and that the language of racial capitalism can be used to "name and analyze the production of social separateness" or the ways in which "forms of humanity are separated (made 'distinct') so that they may be 'interconnected' in terms that feed capital."[41] We have spoken about what Marx called capitalism's "social retort," or the process by which market actors are everywhere and always conscripted into the circulation and accumulation of capital and thus required to participate in competitive social relations that both unite, by putting actors into relation with one another, and divide, by distinguishing winners from losers. The "hidden abode of race," in its secrecy—ever "hidden in plain sight," as Dawson points out—effectively rigs this process by enabling capitalism to make a bloody farce of even a putative commitment to open competition among nominally free market actors. Logics of racialism and capitalism—"historical concomitants," as Robinson and other historians have shown—continue to comingle in fateful ways and effectively *guarantee* that any *ideological* commitment to free and open competition, the apparently progressive and putatively postracial logic of liberal-capitalist social ordering, reproduces racially significant cycles of loss and defeat and fans the flames of racially marked competitive hostilities.[42]

It is perhaps evident already that the theory of *racial* capitalism is also a more overtly *political* theory of capitalism. Consider some of the language and tone that Du Bois adopts in the 1930s, for example, in the references to the "dictatorship of organized industry" and the "counter-revolution of property." *Black Reconstruction* is often heralded, rightly, for its theorization of political subjectivity, the recovery of the revolutionary agency of Black workers, and the self-emancipation of the slaves.[43] But in its account of Black lives, *Black Reconstruction* is neither an epic nor a romance; it is, ultimately, a deeply tragic narrative that underscores the triumph of the counterrevolution, the ways in which "property," the "new and more powerful capitalistic imperialism," beats down its adversaries and upbraids with a new saltiness the already wounded souls of Black people. Where astute critics see the onset of a "silent compulsion of economic relations," Du Bois, that incomparable mediator of wounded souls, sees the decidedly political dictatorship of the White world.

Consider Nikhil Pal Singh's reflection on a passage from Frederick Douglass's 1845 autobiography, which speaks rather prophetically to the political bases of racial capitalism's consolidation and which helps us to think about how the ideology of competition serves and obscures racial domination. "Many of the black carpenters were freemen," Douglass wrote, in a discussion of formal economic competition between the races. "Things seemed to be going on very well. All at once, the white carpenters knocked off, and said they would not work with free colored workmen. Their reason for this, as alleged, was that if free colored carpenters were encouraged, they would soon take the trade into their own hands, and poor white men would be thrown out of employment. My fellow apprentices very soon began to feel it degrading to them to work with me. They began to put on airs, and talk about the 'niggers taking the country,' saying we all ought to be killed."[44] In response to this passage, Singh poses the question: "How does the race-labor conjunction become a race-war conjunction?" His "suspicion," he says, "is that the figure of race-war, far from being an afterthought, in fact controls and mediates the entire sequence that Douglass describes. Indeed, one of the most striking aspects of Douglass's *Narrative* is the way in which he consistently describes slavery as something other than the theft of black labor, emphasizing instead its violent, totalizing claims on black life as a thoroughly militarized and policed social relation." The point, I take it, is that economic competition *appears* to be what drives racial divisiveness, and yet Douglass senses that *behind this appearance* is racial warfare, the belligerent promotion of White supremacy, and in such a context economic competition becomes simply an incendiary device, a weapon to be used in battle. This, I argue, is Du Bois's suspicion, too. Indeed, Singh claims, though without explanation, that "Du Bois would go on to argue [that] the 'real modern labor problem' lies closer to the condition of racial dispossession than to the prospects of normative, wage-earning stability. Capitalist freedoms and their enjoyment (life, liberty, and the pursuit of happiness) in turn require us continuously to 'put on airs' and to cultivate a generous rage against the prospects of a bare life."[45]

As a further testament to this point, consider a passage from Du Bois's earlier period, the well-known and controversial passage from *Darkwater* about how the "discovery of personal whiteness among the world's peoples is a very modern thing, a nineteenth and twentieth century matter, indeed."[46] This passage is more provocative than controversial, for surely Du Bois does not mean to suggest that the emergence of racialism and White supremacy postdate the original sin of African enslavement. This we have discussed. And in contrast to those, such as Walter Johnson, who generalize that this "discovery" is vaguely "recent, a product of the slave trade," I stress the historical precision of Du Bois's reference to the nineteenth and twentieth centuries.[47] Certainly it is no accident that what Du Bois calls the "discovery of *personal* whiteness"—and I highlight, too, the intimacy, the individualism of it—overlaps in his analysis with the onset of the "new capitalism," with the imposition of liberal freedom and the opening, if we can refer to it that way, of the competitive society.[48]

Du Bois goes on to claim that "whiteness" assumes an "ownership of the earth forever and ever," that the embrace of this assumption is what "whiteness" stands for. And he notes that "when the black man begins to dispute the white man's title to certain alleged bequests of the Fathers in wage and position, authority and training . . . when he insists on his human right to swagger and swear and waste," in other words, when Black women and men win their freedom to compete, then "the spell is suddenly broken" and the counterrevolution sets forth "a writing of human hatred, a deep and passionate hatred."[49] What ensues is the ethic of competitive capitalism, the outward saltiness that stirs up perhaps a flavorful friction among those who assume ownership "forever and ever," but that burns like hell in the wounds of the disinherited. Once the counterrevolution of property is complete, "once the industrial class emerged as dominant in the nation," to again quote Robinson, "it possessed not only its own basis of power and the social relations historically related to that power, but it also had available to it the instruments of repression created by the now subordinate southern ruling class." It "could activate racism to divide" and conquer and, Robinson says, "the permutations of the instrument appeared endless: Black against white; Anglo-Saxon against southern and eastern European; domestic against immigrant; proletariat against share-cropper; white American against Asian, Black, Latin American, and so on."[50]

In a 1935 letter to Du Bois, the socialist George Streator, who would go on to write for the *New York Times* as its first Black reporter, claimed that "there is no such thing as a Negro *loving* his race in the matter of capital investment and profit."[51] At least part of the point must have been that capitalism's social form encourages a competitive individualism that all but abolishes the sentimentalism of community, including any appeal to Black nationalism. Du Bois's analysis would seem to underscore this point. But Du Bois's work also underscores the irony that while this competitive individualism, this competitive ethic, may foreclose in advance the prospects for community building on capitalism's underside, it signals a kind of divide-and-conquer strategy that works to the benefit of a certain de facto community of "individuals." For those who assume a kind of personal whiteness, we might say, there surely is such a thing as loving the matter of capital investment and profit.

Conclusion

I have sought to elaborate on the idea that the competitive society ushers in an ethic of privatization, a driving focus on our individual pursuits vis-à-vis those around us, those whom we tend to fear as real or potential threats to our individual development and success. Du Bois always thought of this ethic, this principled focus on individual pursuit, as a product of the White world, a characteristic contribution of what he would refer to in his earlier work as the Teutonic or Anglo-Saxon civilization. At issue is a civilization "built upon the 'Eternal I,'" a civilization for which "the 'high Episcopal Nicene creed,'" its enduring statement of faith, is "'to put heel on neck of man down.'" It is "not that I is above Thee but that I despises Thee."[52] For Du Bois, the great belief of the White world is that we are individuals, and though we are not naturally higher or lower than one another, we find ourselves naturally at odds with one another. The great belief is that the nature of our worldly situation compels our self-interested behavior and that an ethic of privatization is conscripted by a naturally competitive environment.

Du Bois's civilizational argument, which is often dismissed by contemporary readers as a stubborn relic of a nineteenth-century tutelage, is augmented in significant ways by his Depression era reading of Marx. The claim that "the 'high Episcopal Nicene creed' of the Anglo-Saxon is 'to put heel on neck of man down,'" the idea that self-interested behavior is simply a response to an inexorably competitive state of nature, is in some ways a development of Marx's critique of the ideology of classical political economy. In Marx's claim, for example, that Robinson Crusoe, "like a good Englishman, kept a set of books" or that "it is remarkable how Darwin recognizes among beasts and plants his English society with its division of labor, competition, opening up of new markets, 'inventions,' and the Mathusian struggle for existence," we find seeds of Du Bois's claim that the economic principles of Anglo-Saxon civilization, the distinctive and particular ideas of the White world, come to stand in for inexorable human nature and immutable scientific truth.[53] And the takeaway, which shares more than a formal affinity with Marx's point, is that this is ideological bluster, meant to conceal the political imposition of a social form that benefits some but that guarantees loss and defeat for others.

By way of conclusion, I want to return to the speech with which we began this chapter, the 1933 Rosenwald Conference lecture, to address what could be a lingering question about Du Bois's zero-sum realism. Earlier I highlighted Du Bois's insistence that we must "give up the idea that the chief end of an American is to be a millionaire" and that we must "envisage small incomes and limited resources and endless work for the larger goals of life." Du Bois would go on to say, "We must rid ourselves of the persistent idea that the advance of mankind consists of the scaling off of layers who become incorporated with the world's upper and ruling classes, leaving always dead and inert below the ignorant and unenlightened mass of men."[54] These remarks highlight a distinctive feature of Du Bois's political and economic imaginary, what I have referred to throughout as a kind of zero-sum realism, a sense that we are dealing in both victories *and* defeats, that, as Du Bois would remark just three years earlier in another address in Washington, at Howard University, "if civilization is to turn out millionaires, it will also turn out beggars and prostitutes, either at home or among the lesser breeds without law."[55]

Du Bois would have been wary of any attempt to apply bourgeois economic principles to what we might call the racial economy. Within the distribution of the racial hierarchy, it simply makes no sense to speak of aggregate growth and of rising tides fostered somehow by unfettered competition among race groups. Gains for White privilege are only possible when Black lives are made to matter even less. Still, I realize that to invoke the notion of the zero-sum game is to raise some question about the very possibility of aggregate growth in productive capacity and the possibility that the capitalist mode of production can be said to improve basic material standards of living at the macro level. Here it is important to emphasize that Du Bois's thinking appears to align with the big-picture Marxist premise that the development of capitalism reflects a historically unprecedented expansion of human social and productive capacity, that, as Marx and Engels famously put it in *The Communist Manifesto*, the epoch of the bourgeoisie "has been the first to show what man's activity can bring about."[56] As Du Bois would remark in his 1933 address to alumni at Fisk University, "We discovered widely in the eighteenth century and the nineteenth the use of capital and it was a great and beneficent discovery." It was "the rule of sacrificing present wealth for greater wealth to come," and "we produced more wealth than the wealthy could consume." But Du Bois would go on to argue, in what amounts to a further indictment of the liberal form, that we remain beholden to a set of institutional arrangements and a corresponding ideological consciousness that do not allow movement beyond the competitive play of private interest. We "produce primarily for the profit of owners and not for use of the mass of people," and what may be worse for a supposedly democratic society, "we have grown to think that this is the only way in which we can produce."[57]

What I refer to as Du Bois's zero-sum imaginary is not meant to obscure the fact that the consolidation of the capitalist mode of production reflects a heightened capacity for rational control at the level of the human species, at the public or universal level. It is meant to emphasize that such a mode of production remains governed by the competitive interplay of *private* rationalities, by an institutional privileging of *particular* interests. "In the period between 1860 and 1914," Du Bois says, "capitalism had come to its highest development in the European world, and its development meant the control of economic life and with that the domination of political life by the great aggregation of capital." But, he continues, "it became, therefore, increasingly clear, as Karl Marx emphasized at the beginning of the era, that there could be no real democracy unless there was greater economic equality."[58] What I have described as an institutionalized ethic of privatization—which, historically, has been the only approach available to human beings living in relative social isolation and with limited material and technological resources—has become an irrational blockage to the further development of rational capacity at the species level. "There is something radically wrong," Du Bois would say, "with an industrial system that turns out simultaneously paupers and millionaires and sets a world starving because it has too much food."[59] Today our motto remains "Accumulation for the sake of accumulation, production for the sake of production."[60] While the private individual may exhibit a rationality in his own way, adhering to capitalism's regulative principles, throwing himself again and again into circulation in order to maximize return on investment and to protect against the competition, the public as such is rationally adrift, mired in the "despair and debacle of laissez-faire."[61] Some feel this pain more than others.

I have sought to explain Du Bois's evolving sense of disillusionment with the liberal paradigm. With these Depression era reflections on economic structure, this sense of disillusionment may be said to reach its tipping point. But for Du Bois, it is worth noting, all of this is "not, as some [have] assumed, the failure of democracy." It is, he said in the Rosenwald lecture, "the failure of education" and a reflection of the fact that we have "no intelligent democracy upon which we can depend."[62] I turn now to consider some of Du Bois's writings on education and to explore his vision for the Black college as a locus for the critique of the competitive society.

CHAPTER 4

The Black College as a Locus of Critique

The turn to a discussion of education is perhaps to be expected. One of the more resounding refrains of the competitive society is that we must invest in education, in our so-called human capital, to ensure that future generations stand a fighting chance in an increasingly cutthroat global marketplace. And if we lack a commitment to education at the public level, as the terms of the competitive society would seem implicitly to indicate, then certainly as private individuals we are prepared today to claw and scratch, often to the point of bankruptcy, to see that our loved ones receive the competitive advantage that an elite education is thought to afford. This is a standard politician's refrain and a common example of the ethic of privatization. And both, according to the terms of our analysis, are further evidence of a divisive society set up for winners and losers.

What I have identified as an ethic or spirit of privatization is reflective of a kind of democratic obeisance to the liberal paradigm, an abdication of public responsibility in favor of the pursuit of private freedom. True to what Du Bois might have identified as the American theory of compensatory democracy, this preoccupation with our private affairs signals our widespread dependence on both the technical expertise of public administrators and, before that, a broader liberal framework that, as we have indicated, is set up to facilitate private competition. According to Du Bois's analysis, the dependency and powerlessness that we so often experience as ordinary citizens is, as he would put it in 1933, an expression of "the despair and debacle of laissez-faire," a reflection of the fact that our society "has no *intelligent* democracy upon which it can depend." And much of this stems from "the failure of education," from "the stupidity and ignorance of the average voter," from the fact that "we have lied [for] so long about money and business, [that] we do know where the truth is."[1] The point, perhaps germane to any liberal society caught in the throes of economic crisis, is that we tend to raise our citizens to compete as private individuals, to accommodate the practices and ideologies of the competitive society, and without much "honest and earnest criticism" of the public consequences.[2] In other words, our schools do very little to encourage critical consideration of the inequity, the divisiveness, the privatization that competitive interactions yield, and this "failure of education" has a profound impact on the prospects of a responsible and competent democratic public.

Du Bois's writings on education will help us to sketch in a fuller picture of his critique of the competitive society, and I explore in particular Du Bois's vision for the Black college as a locus of critique. Hatched at the onset of the postbellum "new capitalism," plainly integrated into the industrial, financial, and commercial workings of modern society, the Black college, as a *Black* institution, nevertheless remained for Du Bois uniquely situated to cultivate and promote at least something of a transcendent message vis-à-vis that of the White world. As we have seen, Du Bois had long argued that the "Negro race" had to "develop for civilization its particular message, its particular ideal, which shall help to guide the world nearer and nearer that perfection of human life for which we all long, that 'one far-off divine event.'" He had argued that "the full, complete Negro message of the whole Negro race had not yet been given to the world," that Black women and men had to "conserve" the lessons of their shared life experiences as to cultivate a distinctive critical perspective, one that could help to ensure that a genuinely transcendent future, a kind of redemptive countermodernity, was indeed yet to come.[3] And in many ways, the Black college was for Du Bois a principal organ through which this strangely progressive conservationism could potentially manifest itself.

Du Bois was, of course, an academic, twice a professor at the historically Black Atlanta University. He was a popular speaker at various Black schools, including Hampton, Howard, and his alma mater, Fisk University. He would reflect often on the theme of "Negro education," and over time he would sketch in a fairly clear portrait of a series of values or ideals that he thought were appropriate to the mission of the Black college. Among these were hard work, sacrifice, and an "ideal of poverty," which, he noted in 1930, is very nearly the "direct antithesis" to the acquisitive and thus competitive logic of the White world.[4] By itself, this ideal of poverty, of restraint in the pursuit of private wealth accumulation, an ideal conceived by Du Bois as a necessary legacy of a Black college education, could well serve as a basis for a principled critique of the competitive society. But I argue that Du Bois casts a broader vision for how the Black college might facilitate the development of that "full, complete Negro message." I argue that in the 1930s especially, in concert with his growing disillusionment with the liberal paradigm, Du Bois conceives of the Black college as a counsel of universality, an institution uniquely attendant to the struggle for a more sustainable and publicly oriented society, an institution perhaps distinctively situated to expose the particularity of the White world.

It is well known that in the early 1930s, in an apparent about-face on the issue of racial segregation, Du Bois began to argue in favor of what he called a "racial effort," a sort of strategic racial separatism, and it is important to keep in mind that his vision for the Black college, more or less a separatist institution, is part and parcel of an evolving political strategy. "Separate Negro sections will increase race antagonism," Du Bois said in his farewell address to the NAACP in 1934, "but they will also increase economic cooperation, organized self-defense, and necessary self-confidence." And "when all these things are taken into consideration it becomes clearer and clearer to more and more American Negroes that, through voluntary and increased segregation, by careful autonomy and planned economic organization, they may build so strong and efficient a unit that 12,000,000 men can no longer be refused fellowship and equality in the United States." It is tempting to read this—as did, for example, Ralph Bunche, Abram Harris, and many among the younger generation of the 1930s African American intelligentsia—as a turn toward some sort of uplift politics, evidence perhaps of an older Du Bois finally caving to the legacy of Booker T. Washington. But it is crucial to see that for the Du Bois of the 1930s, what separatist institutions like the Black college are to build or to nurture or, as it were, to uplift, is precisely an oppositional stance toward White world ideals and practices, essentially a critical orientation toward the liberal form of the competitive society. "American Negroes must plan for their economic future and the social survival of their fellows," Du Bois said, and they must do so "in the firm belief that this means in a real sense the survival of colored folk in the world and the building of a full humanity instead of a petty white tyranny."[5] The "American Negro can give to the world a new and unique gift," he said a year earlier in the Rosenwald lecture, "an example of intelligent cooperation so that when the new industrial Commonwealth comes," Black people "can go into it as experienced people and not again be left on the outside as mere beggars."[6] Du Bois was never entirely clear on what it would mean to "plan" for a more "cooperative" society. I argue that this uncertainty, what Du Bois in 1940 would identify as the necessary "vagueness of doctrines that attempt universality," is indicative of a speculative dimension of his critical theory. But what is clear, and what was clearly the point for an increasingly anti-American critic, is that the competitive free-for-all of the liberal form is the mark of an insufficiently planned, insufficiently rational White world. It is a social model that allows for a particular few to assume a tyrannical control over a wide range of social losers. Black people know this all too well, Du Bois insists, and the advance and dissemination of this unequivocally political knowledge is, as Du Bois might have put it, the "field and function of the Negro college."

As a disillusioned liberal in the 1930s, Du Bois seems to have concluded that the originary violence of White world segregation had effectively backed Black women and men into the need for a "racial effort," which simply had to include separatist institutions such as the Black college. And for Du Bois this meant precisely that such institutional spaces were to nurture an oppositional message, one based not on any positive claim about racial essentialism, not on any "attempt to validate a biological *race-in-itself*," but rather, as Joel Olson puts it, on "the construction of a *race-for-itself*, a collective united by a common experience of racial subordination and resistance to it."[7] At issue is an oppositional critical and political project, what Bill Mullen has described, invoking Paul Gilroy's famous phrase, as a "mode of passage into a counter-culture of modernity."[8]

"A University of the Air"

Let us revisit the spring of 1933, the moment when Du Bois "began to read and study Karl Marx" and to "supplement the liberalism of Charles Sumner with the new economic contribution of the twentieth century." The signal turning point, Du Bois would say, was a particular speech that he delivered in May of that year to a college audience at Fisk University on the theme of the "Field and Function of the Negro College." That address, along with another given at Fisk in 1938, plainly underscores Du Bois's Depression era disillusionment with the ideals of the White world and it imparts a clear sense that indigenous Black institutions, the Black college in particular, must set afoot "other points of view."[9] Before turning to discuss Du Bois's vision for the Black college as a locus of critique, it will be helpful to revisit his remarks about higher education's role in shaping the object of that critique, the competitive society.

In that 1933 speech in Nashville, Du Bois raised serious concerns about an established model of higher education in the United States, grave concerns about the "kind of university [with which] we are most familiar." At issue is the sort of institution that provides "culture for the cultured," training and knowledge for an elite class and its particular interests, and often despite its advertisements to the contrary. Remarking on this institution's history, Du Bois noted that, "instead of the university growing down and seeking to comprehend in its curriculum the life and experience, the thought and expression of lower classes, it almost invariably tended to grow up and narrow itself to a sublimated elite of mankind." And in this way, "the university [became] cut off from its natural roots and from the mass of men." It became "a university of the air," a kind of echo chamber of ideological consciousness.[10]

It is significant that Du Bois puts this story into historical perspective. He is describing the only kind of college or university that most of us know, and yet, he says, this model is degenerate, a spoiled version of its original self. In what must have been an expression of tremendous heresy, what certainly would be in our time, Du Bois said that the "university, if it is to be firm, must hark back to the original idea of the [West African] bush school," which in its orientation toward the welfare and sustainability of the whole community was a more "perfect system of education."[11] Though he did not elaborate on this assertion, his objective was clear enough. In urging his predominately Black audience to return in spirit to its African past, to an admittedly romanticized image of its bush school, he sought to indicate that the *Black* college, the *Black* university, could set out to redeem a lost sense of universality, and by affirming its distinctive identity in and through persistent exposure of the false universality of the White world. Du Bois told his audience that its charge was precisely to "build the sort of Negro university which [would] emancipate not simply the Black folk of the United States, but those White folk who in their effort to suppress Negroes have killed their own culture—men who in their desperate effort to replace equality with caste and to build inordinate wealth on a foundation of abject poverty have succeeded in killing democracy."[12] Part of the implication, surely, is that the Black college ought to promote a strategy of contestation around the very idea of emancipation. There is something dangerous, even deadly, about how we tend to conceive of freedom in American society and how the "scholarly aloofness and academic calm of most white universities" mistake an interpretation of democratic ideals for the real thing.[13]

Clearly these reflections on the "university of the air" underscore Du Bois's evolving concerns about elitism and class division and the ways in which the nation's colleges and universities, so often cut off from the roots, tend to heed the interests of privileged sons and daughters.[14] These reflections underscore how Du Bois, in 1933, finds himself moving toward a rethinking of the "Talented Tenth," a thesis that he would explicitly and controversially revisit in 1948. Careful observation of Du Bois's writings and scholarly activism from the 1930s reveals that his later, more complicated defense of a sort of college-educated vanguard was decades in the making. We will have occasion to explore this development in the final section of the chapter. But it is important to emphasize here that, in terms of his critique of the competitive society, in this denunciation of "the university of the air," Du Bois underscores the need for an institutional commitment to the practice of ideology critique, a Black college that could expose the production and reproduction of that airy knowledge that sits all too comfortably with the racial and economic status quo.

Consider for a moment Du Bois's long-standing defense of the liberal arts. Appreciation of Du Bois's thinking about college education, like appreciation of so many other dimensions of his thinking, often begins and ends with *The Souls of Black Folk*, where the object of criticism was not how the traditional White colleges and universities practice their craft, not generally with what such schools stand for. The concern, rather, was that Black women and men too often lack access to a traditional liberal arts education and that, at the turn of the twentieth century in the American South, favored voices among the Black elite, principally that of Booker T. Washington and others associated with his "Tuskegee Machine," had sown the seeds of "certain disaster" by promoting vocational training and thereby devaluing the merits of liberal education. For the author of *The Souls of Black Folk*, the liberal arts were taken to reflect the very best of what the White world educational model has to offer.[15]

It is worth pointing out that etymologically the term "liberal arts" refers to an education fit for free men, as opposed to slaves and others of depressed social rank. Raymond Williams has shown that the term's roots can be traced back to early modern Europe, where the term denoted "the skills and pursuits appropriate to men of independent means and assured social position, as distinct from other skills and pursuits (cf., mechanical) appropriate to a lower class."[16] As John Dewey would remark in 1935, in the pages of the *Social Frontier*, the short-lived journal of the Depression era progressive education movement, "a liberal education was [taken to be] the education of a free man. Liberal subjects were those fitted to be pursued by a free man and were opposed to those subjects that were adapted to the training of mechanics."[17] In light of this etymology, it makes perfect sense that the author of *The Souls of Black Folk* would have insisted on a liberal education for freedmen and freedwomen and for the descendants of chattel slaves. As Wendy Brown has noted recently, in a reflection on the role that liberal arts education has played in the cultivation of democratic publics, this sort of education "was necessary for free men to know and engage the world sufficiently to exercise their freedom." In the United States during the early part of the twentieth century, the process of "extending liberal arts education from the elite to the many was nothing short of a radical democratic event, one in which all became potentially eligible for the life of freedom long reserved for the few."[18] Surely Du Bois's efforts to extend liberal arts education across the color line can and should be regarded as the work of a radical democrat. But just as it makes sense for the early Du Bois to extend the liberal arts across the color line, it makes perfect sense, too, that into the 1930s, as a disillusioned liberal and burgeoning reader of Marx, Du Bois would begin to worry about how "most white universities" promote their key terms, how in this case freedom and liberty are being taught to a liberated people.

"Since the early 1900s," notes the historian Derrick Alridge, "Du Bois had advocated a broad educational agenda for blacks that promoted liberal arts at its core." But as "capital aggregations, expanding capital, worldwide credit cartels, and chain stores were taking hold around the globe," as Du Bois began to reckon with the "economic changes" of the 1930s in the way that we have documented, he began "to reassess his educational plan." Du Bois never wavered in his insistence on the liberal arts, on the importance of broad humanistic inquiry, but, increasingly, he sought to promote a model that would go beyond "classical education," a model that would more strongly "encourage students to challenge the status quo."[19] William Watkins has noted that in this period Du Bois came to embrace the Marxist suspicion that, at all levels, American "schools have an ideological purpose," that "their job is to promote individualism, competition," and, generally, "support of Western civilization."[20] If such a civilization stands essentially for the ideals of the classical liberal paradigm, if practices of capital accumulation reflect in essence a White world set in motion, then, as Du Bois would write in 1938, "if these Negro universities have any real meaning it is that in them other points of view should be evolved."[21]

Du Bois lamented the fact that, as he put it, "our best brains are taught and want to be taught in large northern universities where dominant economic patterns and European culture, not only prevail, but prevail almost to the exclusion of anything else."[22] He minced no words in chiding his Fisk audience:

> With few exceptions, we are all today "white folks' niggers." No, do not wince. I mean nothing insulting or derogatory, but this is a concrete designation which indicates that very very many colored folk: Japanese, Chinese, Indians, Negroes; and, of course, the vast majority of white folk; have been so enthused, oppressed, and suppressed by current white civilization that they think and judge everything by its terms. They have no norms that are not set in the nineteenth and twentieth centuries. They can conceive of no future world which is not dominated by present white nations and thoroughly shot through with their ideals, their method of government, their economic organization, their literature and their art; or in others words their throttling of democracy, their exploitation of labor, their industrial imperialism, and their color hate.[23]

Ultimately it was a question of transcendence, a question of what role the Black college would play in moving a multiracial humanity beyond the outmoded terms of a partial civilization. But before that grand question could be answered or even addressed, crucial spadework had to be done. The White world was proving itself to be unsustainable, its core ideals that of a dying civilization. And if Black colleges were going to avoid running their "best brains" over the cliff, they first had to ensure that they were not, as Vincent Harding would put it some years later, simply "dark copies of dying whiteness."[24]

Consider Du Bois's improvisation of "that great line by [Claude] McKay: 'If we must die, let it not be like hogs.'" To his Fisk audience in 1933, Du Bois would insist that "the alternative of not dying like hogs is not that of dying or killing like snarling dogs."[25] The point is that, for the Du Bois of the 1930s, the White university was clear in its mission while the Black college stood at a crossroads. The latter could embrace "what the white world was doing, its goals and ideals."[26] It could embrace a vision of the liberal paradigm, an education for free men in which that freedom amounts to unfettered competition, the art of "dying or killing like snarling dogs." Or it could help to expose the "scholarly aloofness and academic calm of most white universities," the ideological distortions of "the university of the air," and to transcend a model of liberty born and bred in the image of the White world.

"The Neoliberal Arts"

Du Bois points toward challenges that endure into our own time. It may be helpful to offer a few remarks on how the neoliberal era has rolled back the veneer on the competitive society and in a way that underscores the enduring significance of Du Bois's Depression era concerns about the nation's colleges and universities. "Neoliberalism's war on higher education," to borrow Henry Giroux's phrase, is widely acknowledged today.[27] It is widely acknowledged, too, that the liberal arts have become, if not entirely disappeared casualties, at least unwitting conscripts of neoliberal market rationality, increasingly beholden to the drive for capital accumulation and its corresponding ethic of market competitiveness.[28] The liberal arts, like "human capital" or any other commoditized good, finds itself put on the defensive today, compelled to prove its market worth, in this case to students and parents (college administrators might prefer the term "customers"), rankings profilers, peddlers of technology and other "educational products," even state, local, and federal government officials, all of whom have come to think almost exclusively in terms of return on dollar investment.

Much of the literature on the neoliberal assault on higher education conforms to a mythos of decline or degeneration. The presumption is that we have shifted significantly from the historical precedent of a pre-neoliberal landscape, a postwar "middle-class crucible" marked by more widespread investment in public higher education and by the opening of the liberal arts to a broader array of aspiring students. And surely the neoliberal turn has been partly a reaction to the university's role in the postwar empowerment of an unruly and more multiracial middle class, or at least what the traditional American elite has taken to be an emerging political threat. In this the contributions of African American and Chicano student activists and the role of the Black Studies movement of the late 1960s cannot be denied. But again, today's critics of the neoliberal turn usually tell a story of postwar gains followed by Reagan era crisis and subsequent neoliberal decline. And Du Bois rarely if ever factors into this narrative if only because his reflections on higher education antedate the postwar starting premise. During the latter part of his life, Du Bois was far too disillusioned with American society even to anticipate the coming of a 1960s "heyday" for the liberal arts and public higher education. But into the twenty-first century, in the wake of a neoliberal rollback on postwar democratization, Du Bois's time seems to have come again. While his Depression era concerns about the ideology of laissez-faire, about the hegemony of a kind of classical liberal worldview, are undoubtedly products of their time, they seem eerily befitting of a neoliberal moment when, as Christopher Newfield notes, even critics of neoliberal ideas and practices tend to accept the "market as inevitable and irresistible" and embrace the "now-familiar doctrine: American capitalism is here to stay, and in any case it has always been the university's environment."[29] At a time when the culture surrounding higher education "turns the whole of childhood and adolescence into a high-stakes, twelve-year sprint," when our elite, model universities are said to train students "to run faster and faster, so that by the time they finish college, they can make the leap into the rat race," it would seem that our education system has gone to work for precisely the sort of competitive society that Du Bois so feared.[30]

Especially worrisome today is the democratic fallout of the neoliberal turn and the role that higher education continues to play in this. And here Du Bois's reflections are especially generative. Wendy Brown has argued recently that "the saturation of higher education by market rationality has converted higher education from a social and public good to a personal investment in individual futures, futures construed mainly in terms of earning capacity."[31] Henry Giroux has argued similarly: "Democracy can only be sustained through modes of civic literacy that enable individuals to connect private troubles to larger public issues as part of a broader discourse in critical inquiry, dialogue, and engagement," and that neoliberalism has succeeded in "eliminating those public spheres," perhaps most notably the university, "where people learn to translate private troubles into public issues."[32] The concern, in essence, is that American democracy has been reduced to what Du Bois would call its compensatory form, whereby actors are compelled to concern themselves with public life if, and often only if, they can be reasonably confident in a tangible return on their private investment. We have seen these concerns articulated in the pages of *Black Reconstruction*, but before Du Bois even began work on that study he argued, in his 1933 speech at Fisk, that "the citizen of a democracy who thinks of democratic government chiefly as a means of his own advancement, meets and ought to meet disappointment. Only insofar as he conceives of democracy as the only way to advance the interests of the mass of people, even when those interests conflict with his, is he playing the role of the patriot."[33] Brown and Giroux's point would be that our schools, our colleges and universities especially, can and should help maturing citizens to reflect on and dialogue about "the interests of the mass of people." Their point would be that in this our present system of higher education falls short, that today, by and large, our institutions of advanced learning do not give young people the tools and motivation to "translate private troubles into public issues." If anything, our schools do precisely the opposite, by promoting a culture of entrepreneurial individualism in which students and faculty alike are rewarded for translating public issues, "the interests of the mass of people," into private concerns and investment-worthy enterprises. Let the competition begin.

One could go on about the neoliberal assault on higher education and the extent to which today's colleges and universities have become conscripts of the competitive society. My point is simply that we can draw meaningful connections between our moment and Du Bois's, that his Depression era concerns about higher education are generative for our thinking about enduring features of an American society set up to facilitate private competition. Today critics argue that in so many ways the neoliberal university "has generated a caste system: 'winners and losers,' 'makers and takers,' 'the best and the brightest.'"[34] Du Bois, in 1933, would take issue with the complicity of higher education in a "desperate effort to replace equality with caste and to build inordinate wealth on a foundation of abject poverty." This effort, he said, had essentially "succeeded in killing democracy." So what of the Black college?

"The Vagueness of Doctrines That Attempt Universality"

"This may be a dream," he said, "but it is worth considering."[35] What Du Bois had in mind was nothing short of a revolutionary institution, though this vision appears far less fantastic when it is seen as an expression of a critical theoretical project, part of a spadework effort to expose the limitations of the competitive society. The Black college had to be, simply by virtue of its demographic, more intimately connected than its White counterpart to the life and death struggles of the competitive society. It was an institution that, in its pedagogy and scholarship, in its fostering of student and alumni communities, would take its cues from the lived realities of the masses of Black women and men. "The American Negro problem is and must be the center of the Negro university," Du Bois said. "Plans for the future of our group, must be built on a base of our problems, our dreams and frustrations; they cannot stem from empty air or successfully be based on the experiences of others."[36] And crucially, as this latter passage indicates, there was to be an emphasis on planning. The competitive society left too much to chance. The "reactionary economics of Northern schools" made too many human beings into snarling dogs or at least citizens who aspire to "become incorporated with the world's upper and ruling classes, leaving always dead and inert below the ignorant and unenlightened mass of men."[37] In his speeches and writings on the Black college, Du Bois sought to make an intellectual case for the kind of criticism that would expose the false universality of the White world or what he seems to have regarded as the insufficiently rational character of the competitive society. In this section, the first of two on Du Bois's portrayal of what he thought had to be distinctive attributes of the Black college, I focus on what I call the speculative dimension of the institutional mission, or the way in which the critical work of the Black college is to be animated and sustained by an implicit and necessarily underdetermined narrative account of "social reconstruction."

In 1940, Du Bois said that his writings and speeches on education often reflected "the vagueness of doctrines that attempt universality."[38] This phrase captures something of this speculative dimension to which I refer. Rather than affirm the status quo, Du Bois sought to negate it. And he did so through an appeal to something more universal, an idea of a future world that may not be entirely articulable, at least not yet, but that would seem to betray a negation of the "despair and debacle of laissez-faire," a movement beyond a mere free play of particular interests and private rationalities. Du Bois's critique is borne along by a sense that the competitive society is, if not irrational, at least insufficiently rational, and that what it would mean to work toward "social reconstruction"—and here I hone in on a trope that figures so prominently in Du Bois's work, and that of other progressive theorists, during the 1930s—is precisely to expose this insufficiency, to find fault with it, to stir up protest against it. This negative criticism of the present is vivified in and through a contrast with a speculative beyond, what Du Bois occasionally refers to as the "dream" of a more comprehensively planned society. Again, there is a certain "vagueness" here, as there must be. At one point, Du Bois refers simply to "the Impossible Must."[39] My point is that Du Bois employs, and in his writings on the Black college perhaps principally as a kind of rhetorical strategy, a sense that we find ourselves participating in a development narrative, an ongoing expansion of our rational capacity as a human species, and this broader narrative helps to vivify the untruth, the irrationality, the unreconstructed character of our present moment.

Here it will be helpful to recount briefly Du Bois's appropriation of the Marxist theory of rational development. I have suggested that Du Bois appears implicitly to endorse the Marxist notion that the onset of the capitalist mode of production, along with the emergence of a broadly liberal political apparatus, signals a historically unprecedented expansion of human social and productive capacity. For Marx, this historical unfolding is consistent with the development of human rationality. At issue is the capacity to control our worldly situation through the exploitation of natural resources and the coordination of human labor. And for Marx, the dawn of the industrial revolution, the advent of the bourgeois age, has been a remarkably revelatory event. But in this period, our period, significant contradictions remain. These are irrational, unsustainable contradictions. An unprecedented capacity to produce, to distribute, to communicate is met with the persistence of widespread poverty, segregation, selfishness. The problem, for Marx, is that our culture, our ideas, what he refers to as our "legal and political superstructure," has become a set of ideological "fetters," irrational obstacles to the further development of productive and social capacity. Liberal culture, the ideological instrument of the bourgeoisie, has encouraged us to think of human freedom and rational development in terms of state protection of individual rights. Such an approach might give *private* individuals a degree of *private* rationality, a freedom or opportunity to control what they can. In this, some fare better than others. But when it comes to problems of broad *public* concern, unless enough propertied individuals can be persuaded to volunteer their time and money, unless enough "winners" can be persuaded to help enough "losers," the "interests of the mass of people" simply go unaddressed. There is very little semblance of what we might call *public* rationality, or a shared capacity to control outcomes at the public level. And according to the terms of modern liberal culture, such public failures are often chalked up simply to chance misfortune. They are taken to be the tragic derivatives of an all-too-human starting point, that inexorably competitive state of nature.

In the development narrative undergirding this line of social criticism, many will see a trace of Enlightenment rationalism. There is an unmistakable emphasis on purposive control over chance and contingency. And this idea that we ought to try to harness our human power to control has too often been used as a way to rationalize or explain away widespread brutality and exploitation. But the general narrative of rational development, the idea that we have to plan and coordinate our energies and resources simply to make our world livable, is not to be confused with what Du Bois decries as the characteristic contribution of the White world, which is decidedly liberal and in many ways the same object of the Marxist critique.[40] Of course, Du Bois was concerned that even the most progressive of the European critics were ill-prepared to grasp how "the discovery of personal whiteness" could and would be used to extend the shelf life of the liberal form. "It would have been exceedingly difficult," Cedric Robinson has said, referring to the racial myopia of European radicalism, "and most unlikely that a [European] civilization in its ascendancy as a significant power in the world would produce a tradition of self-examination sufficiently critical to expose one of its more profound terms of order."[41] But the Du Bois of the 1930s might have said, anticipating Frantz Fanon, that this is precisely why we need critics who can give us a "slightly stretched" version of Marxist analysis.[42]

Notice how Du Bois employs something of the Marxist development narrative in, for example, his 1941 charge to the students and faculty at Lincoln University in Missouri. "You have an extraordinary opportunity," he said, "not so much for social imitation and social conflict, but rather for social invention, for planning and carrying through methods by which, without hatred, agitation, or upheaval, you can show how a minority can not simply repeat the accomplishments of a majority, but can show the majority the way of life." In doing this, Du Bois said, "You but reiterate an age-old custom that not from the overwhelming, rich, and powerful groups which from time to time rule the world have come salvation and culture, but from the still small voice of the oppressed and the determined who knew more than to die and plan more than mere survival." Du Bois stressed that "the Negroes of Missouri" were standing at a critical juncture, that in the midst of enduring hardship many will be tempted to "sell their votes not for the establishment of a state university but for small offices and temporary refinement, for the paying of personal debts and squaring of personal dislikes and enmities, rather than for the larger and more intangible object of building here a center of thought and speculation, of scientific research, and of literature and art." The Black college could become, he said, "a center where the culture of this country is to be changed and uplifted and helped in the reconstruction of the world."[43] The clear insinuation, in these admittedly vague references to planning and speculation and the reconstruction of society, is that extant reality reflects only a very limited application of our human capacity to control our worldly situation. Real is the temptation to settle in, to get for ourselves a little foothold in a world marked by opportunity for private rationality, a puncher's chance in the struggle for "mere survival." But real, too, is the speculative possibility of further development, the building of a more universal, more public rationality.[44]

The language of reconstruction is revealing. This language figures prominently in Du Bois's writings on education throughout the 1930s. In the spring of 1935, for example, the Howard University philosopher Alain Locke persuaded Du Bois to contribute a volume to his "Bronze Booklets" series of adult education textbooks, an initiative sponsored by an emerging group known as the Associates in Negro Folk Education and underwritten by the Carnegie Corporation.[45] Du Bois was skeptical, given Alain Locke's liberal leanings, and ultimately, thanks to the initiative's corporate backing, which was unknown to Du Bois at the time, the proposed contribution was deemed too radical for publication. That contribution was entitled "The Negro and Social Reconstruction," and a portion of it, what came to be known as the "Basic American Negro Creed," would be published in a column in 1936 and then again four years later, in the final chapter of *Dusk of Dawn*. In this text, as elsewhere, Du Bois proffered what were then familiar leftist tropes of the "planned economy" and faith in the "ultimate triumph of some form of Socialism the world over," what he described simply as the coming of a "common ownership and control of the means of production." He claimed that "if carefully and intelligently planned, a co-operative Negro industrial system in America can be established in the midst of and in conjunction with the surrounding national industrial organization and in

intelligent accord with that reconstruction of the economic basis of the nation which must sooner or later be accomplished."[46] It is significant and precisely to my point that—as in the Lincoln address and in his other speeches
on education that "attempt universality"—Du Bois does not provide any
substantive argumentation for how exactly such economic and social "reconstruction" might come about, how such a transcendent or ultimately
universal future could or would be "carefully and intelligently planned." But
Du Bois is writing to and for adult learners, essentially college students.
And in his writings on education, in his speeches to college students, Du
Bois almost invariably invokes the rhetorical mode of the charge. The idea
is not to give the audience all the answers, not to shut down critical and creative thinking; rather, the idea is to vivify the urgency of a task, to inspire the
audience to take up that task and to figure out how best to work through
it. As we see in the Lincoln speech, in his would-be Bronze Booklets contribution, and in so many of his Depression and World War II era works on
the Black college, that task includes a critical negation of a liberal society
marked by a false sense of universality, a society in desperate need of reconstruction. That teardown project requires a vision of a more rational control
over the public domain. The crucial point, for our purposes, is that the appeal to reconstruction, to a more "carefully and intelligently planned" society and economy, serves a speculative function. Take nothing for granted.
Heed the truth of the unbuilt. Work toward the Impossible Must.

Du Bois was not alone in his emphasis on "social reconstruction" as a
guiding theme of a more progressive educational model, though he was
far more distinctive in his attentiveness to the "Negro problem" and in his
insistence on the leading role that the Black world could play in advanc-
ing the cause. The intellectuals behind the more widely known progressive
education movement of the 1930s—figures such as George Counts, Merle
Curti, William Heard Kilpatrick, and John Dewey—fashioned themselves
as "Social Reconstructionists." Their short-lived journal, the *Social Frontier*,
contained editorials and essays that lamented the Depression era establishment of a classically liberal common sense and that often appealed to a
more rationally planned social and economic structure. In striking comparison to what I described in the previous chapter as the postbellum consolidation of capitalism's social form, the journal's inaugural editorial started
from the premise that "new forms of communication, transformation, and
production, [had] literally destroyed the individualistic economy of the

early years of the republic" and that "in place of the relatively independent and self-contained households and rural neighborhoods of the Jeffersonian era, the American people stand today before a vast and complicated economic mechanism embracing the entire country and reaching out to the far corners of the globe—a fait accompli having the most revolutionary consequences." Like Du Bois, the Social Reconstructionists—or "Frontiersmen," as they were also known in reference to the title of their journal—sought a future world that would be more "dependent . . . on the planful and rational character of technology," a world that would "demand more and more of coordination and unified direction and control."[47] Like Du Bois, they grew increasingly disillusioned with a New Deal strategy that, by 1935, had "shifted toward restoring an economically competitive society."[48] And, like Du Bois, they sought to challenge an American academy that had become an echo chamber for decidedly liberal theories of freedom. In 1935, for example, the education reformer Harold Rugg wrote of a "hiatus between the content of American scholarship and the vital problems of the people," which he attributed largely to "the fact that the rank and file of American scholars are molded into defenders of the status quo by the dominant social milieu in which they have been brought up, and by the special concepts of their own intellectual climate." Professional academics tended to be "members of the upper middle class," he noted, the "sons of native stock and are possessors of a small property and of prestige in the community," and "true to the American tradition, they are thoroughgoing individualists and practice the concept of freedom to compete and—many of freedom to exploit." On the whole, they are

> still convinced that, even in the new industrialism, the ladder of opportunity really stretches upward before anyone who conforms, works hard, saves, and invests. Their economic-social creed is a synthesis of the concepts of the First Industrial Revolution. Outstanding among these are: scarcity, laissez-faire, building for immediate profits, accelerating growth, production for sale, and a hierarchy of social classes in which the entrepreneur and the politician occupy the loftiest positions and the creative person is either ignored or held in contempt.[49]

Though these remarks were crafted and published some eighty years ago, they could pass as biting criticism of the neoliberal academy in the twenty-first century.[50]

William Watkins has noted that "the Social Reconstructionists never claimed Du Bois, nor did he claim them," but "they were undeniably linked by virtue of their history, pedagogy, and views on the nature of society, Socialism, and reform." Watkins has noted, too, that the "Reconstructionists" were not blind to race, that "their larger work suggests an interest in the 'Negro question' and specifically the education of Blacks."[51] In one notable piece published in the *Social Frontier*, an essay entitled "The Problem of Minorities," the pioneering sociologist Margaret Mead spoke, if only in passing, to the driving theme of our analysis. "Race prejudice rages most fiercely," she said, "in those areas of society where economic competition is the strongest and in those periods of depression when economic anxiety is the deepest."[52] So Du Bois was not alone in his thinking about progressive education; his emphasis on planning, on the trope of "social reconstruction," bore the markers of its time, discernable traces of a broader Depression era intellectual milieu. But Du Bois's insistence that "the American Negro problem is and must be the center of the Negro university," that "plans for the future of our group, must be built on a base of our problems, our dreams and frustrations," lends a distinctive gravity to the kind of critique that Du Bois sought to institutionalize. And, as I have tried to suggest here, we can learn something about the nature of this critique by studying the way that Du Bois makes his case for its institutionalization. The rhetorical mode of the charge—the charge to the graduates, we might say—taps into a speculative dimension. In its necessary "vagueness," this speculative gesture underscores the irrationality of the inherited world and its competitive form, and also the subsequent need not to accommodate this inheritance, but actively to negate it.

"A Clear Vision of Present World Conditions and Dangers"

At this point, it is necessary to remark on Du Bois's elitism, as his later critical theory is ambivalent about both the epistemic status of the critique and the question of who is fit to carry it out. Colleges and universities, whether PWIS or HBCUS or other so-called MSIS ("Minority-Serving Institutions"), are and have been elite spaces, to greater or lesser degrees, and while the later Du Bois came to lament conventional scholarly detachment from the masses, his critical theory of the 1930s remained anchored in the assumption of certain epistemic privilege. It is less a critical theory understood as a "self-clarification . . . of the struggles and wishes of the age," to quote the very early Marx, and more that of a "man at last compelled to face with so-ber senses his real conditions of life," to quote the Marx engaged in a more confident *Ideologiekritik*.[53] Du Bois's resistance to the competitive society is born of a refined epistemic vantage, what he would describe, in his best at-tempt at his least elitist voice, as "a clear vision of present world conditions and dangers."[54] When the ideologies of the competitive society run deep, as they did in Du Bois's time and as they do in ours, the work of evolving "other points of view," for Du Bois the essential mission of the Black college, re-quires a cultivated suspicion, and not merely self-clarification, of the strug-gles and wishes of the age.

Earlier I mentioned that Du Bois's reconsideration of the Talented Tenth was decades in the making. "It is sometimes forgotten," Nikhil Singh re-minds us, "that Du Bois left the NAACP in 1934 because he thought it had be-come an overly centralized, top-heavy organization devoted to elitist bro-kerage politics, rather than to direct organizing among a black mass base."[55] When he put forth his formal reconsideration of the Talented Tenth thesis in a 1948 speech to the Grand Boulé Conclave of Sigma Pi Phi at Wilberforce University in Ohio, Du Bois reinforced many of the themes that had domi-nated his writings of the 1930s. Assuming again the mode of the charge, he described a speculative unfolding of a rationalist development narrative, a "reconstruction" fashioned not by aristocrats, but by the masses of women and men, those whom he described as the "real people," whose further de-velopment of the "possibilities of human effort" were fit to expose the un-truth of the present moment, the "real people" who stood poised to "build something better."[56] Once again, Du Bois lamented the cozy relationship between the nation's conventional "schools and universities" and the reac-tionary economics of the "industrial interests, which have tried desperately to make Americans turn back to the belief of the eighteenth and nineteenth centuries, that free individual enterprise, with the least possible social con-trol and spurred mainly by the incentive of private profit, is the only method which can bring and preserve prosperity." And, in what marks the distinc-tiveness and namesake of the speech, Du Bois proposed as a way forward a "new idea for the Talented Tenth: the concept of a group-leadership, not simply educated and self-sacrificing, but with clear vision of present world conditions and dangers, and conducting American Negroes to alliance with culture groups in Europe, America, Asia and Africa, and looking toward a new world culture." This was a "new idea" of "group-leadership," Du Bois said, but in this gesture toward a more reciprocal relationship between leaders and the "group," in this move toward a kind of give and take model in which it is not always clear who leads whom, one senses perhaps a trace of Du Bois's famous claim, put forth in *The Souls of Black Folk*, that the very "soul of democracy" consists in sober criticism "of government by those governed, of leaders by those led."[57]

Stephanie Shaw has argued that Du Bois's original proposal for a Talented Tenth leadership class, first articulated in 1903, was more progressive than scholars have acknowledged and that his 1948 reconsideration was not a rejection of his earlier elitism but rather a more contextually measured defense of a group-leadership model that would negate and potentially transcend the worst of what passed for educated leadership in American bourgeois society. Shaw argues that while many readers of Du Bois have regarded his later "incorporation of socialist ideas as an indication of his radicalization and his moving away from the Talented Tenth ideal, he was especially emphatic in his support [of the thesis] in this second iteration," that his "move toward Marxism" might better "reflect his expanding, internationalizing, or in today's parlance, globalizing, rather than retreating from, his original proposal."[58] Shaw's point is important in that there will remain a certain distinctiveness to the cultivated space of the Black college, that whatever leadership potential a midcentury Du Bois would begin to identify in the Black working class, the college-educated—which, throughout Du Bois's lifetime, remained less than 10 percent of the Black US population—would have a role to play, though only to the extent that they could sustain a requisite self-awareness and the courage not only to resist the trappings of privilege but also to challenge a model of society built on its reproduction.[59]

That self-awareness was precisely what Du Bois did not see in either the membership of the Grand Boulé or the "sycophantic and cowardly leadership" of many midcentury Black educational institutions.[60] Du Bois's reconsidered defense of a college-educated leadership class was thus grounded in a rejection of the "exclusiveness and snobbery" that had come to be associated with the Talented Tenth, a rejection of the ways in which a college-bred elite had been taught to cloak itself in the privatizing and competitive ethos of the liberal form.[61] I mentioned earlier, in reference to the 1933 speech at Fisk, that Du Bois saw in the Black college the possibility of an institution that could "grow down to the roots" rather than up to the airy detachment of a sublimated elite. A decade earlier, in the mid-1920s, in early correspondence with Abram Harris, Du Bois entertained ideas about a more popular alternative even to the Black colleges and universities, what he and Harris imagined as a "New Spirit College" for Black working people, a kind of "politically active worker's college."[62] In that same decade, Du Bois promoted student activism against what had become a reactionary administration at Fisk, a reality he had been made privy to largely through correspondence with then-student, and later *Crisis* operative, George Streator.[63] Into the 1930s and through the Second World War, Du Bois promoted an initiative known as the People's College, first as a national board member and then, with the sociologist Ira De A. Reid, as a founder and instructor at the People's College at Atlanta University. That initiative sought to open the doors of college classrooms and faculty offices to interested adult learners, regardless of their prior level of educational attainment or ability to pay. In Atlanta in the early 1940s, Du Bois offered free classes on African history and civilization.[64] But while Du Bois may have promoted student activism and autonomy, while he sought to challenge the exclusionary or gated character of the traditional academy through an appeal to more porous campus boundaries, he did not exactly throw himself over in earnest to the new "group-leadership" model. For the later Du Bois, that give-and-take relationship between town and gown remained hierarchically structured in a notable way.

In 1971, at the height of the Black Studies movement in North American higher education, Vincent Harding published a remarkable essay entitled "Toward the Black University," in which he channeled at least part of the legacy of Du Bois's later vision for the Black college. Harding imagined an arrangement in which "the boundaries of the community and the boundaries of the university would be constantly blurred," in which "the art and literature and basic survival wisdom found in the off-campus community would be welcomed on the campus as part of the mutual learning experience."[65] One is reminded here of Harding's contemporary Walter Rodney, the Afro-Guyanese scholar-activist who argued, in his 1969 *The Groundings with My Brothers*, that the Black intellectual must shun petit bourgeois detachment and instead "attach himself to the activity of the Black masses."[66] For Rodney, as for Harding, only this kind of popular groundedness, only this sort of comradely solidarity with the self-activity of the people, could yield truly revolutionary scholarship, teaching, and learning. But to this 1960s model of critical pedagogy, to this more radical scholar-activist attachment to the autonomous struggles of the disinherited, the Du Bois of the 1930s was prepared to meet only halfway, and for better or for worse. Even in his least elitist moments, Du Bois seems to have been less interested than Harding or Rodney in counseling the "street wisdom" of the off-campus community. For Du Bois, the idea was simply to listen to the voices of off-campus communities, to embrace "street wisdom" as testimony, as evidence in support of a foregone starting premise. The idea was simply to help show how the lived realities of such communities vivify the "despair and debacle of laissez-faire," the worst of a competitive society torn between winners and losers. I have suggested throughout this book that the later Du Bois engaged in old-fashioned ideology critique, and one insinuation is that Du Bois tended to traffic in diagnoses of false consciousness. Though he appears never to have used this specific language, he worried frequently about the seductiveness of White world ideas and about the ways in which, in this case, off-campus communities tacitly consent to their own oppression through subscription to liberal ideas. He worried intensely about a people who, to quote again the 1938 speech at Fisk, "have been so enthused, oppressed, and suppressed by current white civilization that they think and judge everything by its terms." To be sure, Du Bois moved delicately here. But clearly the Black college classroom was meant to provide, with requisite authority, something of a ministering hand.

To this point, it is worth noting that Du Bois often referred to the Black college as a vehicle of propaganda, a platform on which to project what he called the "unified cultural message," or what I might identify rather as a consolidated political message.[67] "One of the central characteristics of the Black University movement," Harding said, in a remark that is absolutely consistent with Du Bois's legacy, "is its willingness to define education as being unashamedly political."[68] And to the possible concern that this renders the vision shallow, that there is something off-putting, some might say *illiberal*, about a sense that the Black college is and ought to be a partisan operation, I stress two points. One is that the more worrisome partisan operation, for Du Bois, is to be found in the curriculum and training put on by White world institutions. We are quick to judge as narrow or shallow any Black counterpropaganda, yet we remain unwilling even to entertain the thought that our conventional system of adult education, built almost exclusively by and for the White world, is often, as Du Bois put it, "education propaganda for things as they are."[69] The second point is that Du Bois never insisted that students and faculty at Black colleges must, as it were, toe a *positive* party line. In his emphasis on the rhetorical mode of the charge and its speculative "vagueness," Du Bois envisioned an institutional space that, taken as a whole, would foster a critical spirit born of a persistent and sober-senses assessment of the "Negro problems." Such an assessment would require a "growing down to the roots," a driving and sustained attentiveness to the societal losses stacked up in and around Black communities at the hands of the liberal form. But while Du Bois assumed that such an assessment, itself broad in scope and open to a wide range of contributions, would necessarily yield "other points of view," it is fundamental to the nature of the mission, indeed to the nature of Du Bois's critical theory, that a singular and authoritative voice, that Du Bois's own voice, not proffer a positive determination of what exactly those other points of view would entail. What is far more determined, for a disillusioned Du Bois of the 1930s, is the mission's starting premise, the *negative* or *diagnostic* stance, rather than any more positive or prescriptive one.

Here it will be helpful to underscore once again the category of the disillusioned liberal. Du Bois's vision for the Black college is most certainly a product of its historical context. His Depression era disillusionment with a liberal model of society had a profound effect on his sense for why an oppositional institution was needed, what lives and experiences might inform that institution, what that institution might stand for. "Here we stand," Du Bois said to his Fisk audience in 1933. "We are American Negroes. It is beside the point to ask whether we form a real race. Biologically we are mingled of all conceivable elements, but race is psychology, not biology; and psychologically we are a unified race with one history, one red memory, and one revolt." He would go on to say, or indeed to *ask*, in good speculative form: "Our problem: How far and in what way can we consciously and scientifically guide our future so as to insure our physical survival, our spiritual freedom and our social growth? Either we do this or we die."[70] The White world had created the need for the Black college. Under Black world leadership, that creation "is and is designed to be a program of racial effort," Du Bois said, but such a "narrowed goal [is] forced upon us today by the unyielding determination of the mass of the white race to enslave, exploit, and insult Negroes."[71] These are the words of a disillusioned critic, one who finds himself backed into a program of "racial effort," but who is convinced that force of circumstance had shaped a "real people" who, through "unified cultural message," through a heeding of the "main job" of the Black college, are poised to expose and ultimately abolish a false reality set up to protect the victories and legacies of a precious few.[72] Du Bois seems to imagine, in other words, an institution that is committed and unyielding in its condemnation of the White world, but that "welcome[s] all men of all colors so long as their subscription to this basic creed is sincere and is proven in their deeds."[73]

Angela Davis, a contemporary critic working very explicitly in the tradition of the later Du Bois, has given us a way of thinking about Black struggle and political organization that is, I think, quite instructive. Davis says that in the contemporary world, now more than a half-century after Du Bois's death, "across all the complicated lines of politics and class, it would be futile to try to create a single black community today." But in this neoliberal moment it makes sense to "think about organizing communities" and "not simply around their blackness, but primarily around political goals. Political struggle has never been so much a question about how it is identified or chooses to identify as it has been a question of how one thinks race, gender, class, sexuality affect the way human relations are constructed in the world."[74] The critique of the competitive society takes dead aim at the way human relations are constructed in the world. Behind what Du Bois calls the "Negro problems" we might locate as a kind of metaproblem the way in which the liberal form requires the competitive positing of ascriptive differences of all kinds. On Du Bois's account, the Black college is concerned less with how one is identified or chooses to identify than it is with how one thinks or is charged to think about competitive social relations, the structural form of a dying world. "Dark copies of dying whiteness," Harding said, "are no longer needed."

Conclusion

In 2013, President Barack Obama gave a charge to the graduates of one of the nation's most esteemed Black colleges. Speaking at Morehouse College in Atlanta, Obama unwittingly did his best to repudiate the legacy of Du Bois. In a rather regrettable twist of phrase, he offered essentially a warm embrace of a coldly competitive society:

I understand there's a common fraternity creed here at Morehouse: "Excuses are tools of the incompetent used to build bridges to nowhere and monuments of nothingness." Well, we've got no time for excuses. Not because the bitter legacy of slavery and segregation have vanished entirely; they have not. Not because racism and discrimination no longer exist; we know those are still out there. It's just that in today's hyperconnected, hypercompetitive world, with millions of young people from China and India and Brazil—many of whom started with a whole lot less than all of you did—all of them entering the global workforce alongside you, nobody is going to give you anything that you have not earned. Nobody cares how tough your upbringing was. Nobody cares if you suffered some discrimination. And moreover, you have to remember that whatever you've gone through, it pales in comparison to the hardships previous generations endured—and they overcame them. And if they overcame them, you can overcome them, too.[75]

It is remarkable how far the neoliberal presidency has come. Contrast President Lyndon Johnson's commencement remarks at Howard University in 1965. "You do not take a person who, for years, has been hobbled by chains and liberate him, bring him up to the starting line of a race and then say, 'you are free to compete with all the others,' and still justly believe that you have been completely fair," Johnson said. "It is not enough just to open the gates of opportunity. All our citizens must have the ability to walk through those gates."[76] Nowadays the president of the United States is compelled to announce the tragic fact that the competitive society is here to stay. And nobody cares or ought to care. Deal with it.[77] A half century prior, the same officeholder could not muster the courage to espouse White world ideology in such stark terms, but even Johnson's seemingly warmer remarks paid tribute to the competitive society in a way that Du Bois would vehemently contest.[78] The worry, on this reading, is that competition guarantees loss and defeat for some, and even if we could commit to a practice of something like fair competition, something like a genuine equality of opportunity, the competitive form necessarily promotes a privatizing ethos that feeds on the exploitation of racial and other ascriptive differences.

Heeding this premise, the Black college can and must provide a more radical intervention. Its mission, or a fundamental part of it, is precisely to articulate these critical concerns. To be sure, Du Bois had no illusions about the revolutionary potential of educational reform alone. "If we are to expect the school to change the basis of our economic life, rationalize our religion, balance our psychological impulses and in general guide our society, we are wrong," he said in 1935.[79] Ever wary of silver-bullet solutions, "ever the dialectician," as Alridge points out, "Du Bois was cautious about the ability of schools to bring about full democracy, arguing that a transformation of economic and political institutions was equally necessary to change the social order."[80] Still, Du Bois was compelled to make his arguments about the Black college, just as Harding was compelled to make his case for the Black university, because Black schools can easily replicate the worst of the White world. In our time, this threat is perhaps omnipresent.

Today's Black colleges and universities are struggling not just as institutions driven to court private philanthropy through a toeing of the neoliberal line, but by students and faculties who are compelled, not by weakness of character but by the sheer weight of the neoliberal order, to situate their work within the American theory of compensatory democracy, a theory that is proving to be quite durable indeed. Too many today struggle to step back and critique structure, concerned as they are, indeed as we all are, "with the challenges of being isolated and surviving at the bottom of a savage neoliberal order." As Henry Giroux and Michael Dawson point out, "neoliberalism's 'best trick' is to persuade individuals, as a matter of common sense, that they should 'imagine [themselves] as . . . solitary agent[s] who can and must live the good life promised by capitalist culture."[81] If he were around today, Du Bois would be deeply concerned about the Black college's dependence on White philanthropy.[82] He would most certainly rebuke the widespread turn to "entrepreneurship" as the perceived golden ticket, the surefire vehicle for rendering the Black college "investment worthy" and its students labor ready. He would surely rebuke the rising cost of higher education, which is so often tied today to the perceived need to "compete" for rankings, often through the provision of amenities, such as luxurious dormitories and lavish sports facilities, that are entirely unrelated to any would-be progressive educational mission of the college. For Du Bois, and I will end with this very telling remark, "Two things and only two things are necessary—teachers and students. Buildings and endowments may help, but they are not indispensible."[83] The Impossible Must.

CHAPTER 5

Honoring Dr. Du Bois

"He was in the first place a teacher," Martin Luther King Jr. said in a stirring 1968 tribute to Du Bois. "He would have wanted his life to teach us something about our tasks of emancipation." To a Carnegie Hall audience, on the occasion of what would have been Du Bois's one hundredth birthday, King described his predecessor as a scholar-activist who found himself pressed into battle and who regarded Black teaching and learning as the weapon of choice. "He had to deal with the army of white propagandists, the myth-makers of Negro history," King said, and "one idea that he insistently taught was that black people have been kept in oppression and deprivation by a poisonous fog of lies that depicted them as inferior, born deficient, and deservedly doomed to servitude to the grave." King went on to praise *Black Reconstruction*, in particular. He underscored Du Bois's efforts there to cut through conventional accounts of the Reconstruction period and to vivify "the Negroes' capacity to govern and fitness to build a finer nation in a creative relationship with poor whites."[1]

What King referred to as a "fog of lies," or rather the way that King described the persistence of typical White world falsehoods, underscores the historical consolidation of the competitive society and its sustaining ideologies. Toward the end of his life, King had become a disillusioned liberal, too. His critique of capitalism had grown more amplified. He had become more outspoken in his criticism of the ways in which ideas about equal opportunity and individual responsibility, the purportedly color-blind ideals of the competitive society, were being made to undermine the struggle for a more fundamental redistribution of wealth and income, what King had come to regard as the material sine qua non of the Black freedom struggle. This is perhaps most evident in "King's growing disillusionment with the War on Poverty," which, as the historian Thomas Jackson has documented, "became marked in late 1965," just months after Lyndon Johnson had trumpeted his embrace of the competitive society to the graduating class at Howard University. King saw promise in Great Society programs that were "meant to eradicate welfare dependency," but he watched in distress as they became "increasingly identified with welfare and the undeserving black poor."[2] The same "fog of lies" that Du Bois and others had fought to demystify was being made to nurture the same old vision of society, a model built on the presupposition of winners and losers.[3] In his contribution to the 1965 annual report of the Southern Christian Leadership Conference (SCLC), King warned that without a more radical challenge to the competitive model, any "war on poverty" would be for naught, as "black and white workers at the bottom of the economic ladder will be thrown [right back] into fierce competition for disappearing jobs, giving rise to destructive racial tensions and perhaps violence."[4]

Although King did not live through the capital accumulation crises of the 1970s, one can imagine how he might have responded to the endurance of the competitive form through deindustrialization and into the contemporary era of neoliberal austerity. "There is nothing more dangerous," he said in 1966, "than to build a society with a large segment of individuals in that society who feel that they have no stake in it, who feel that they have nothing to lose."[5] While today's "surplus populations" are still composed disproportionately of people of color, their status is not always framed in terms of battles over disappearing jobs or even in terms of competition at all. What Michael Denning has called "wageless life" seems to have been written off in a new way, as a devalued population that is woefully uncompetitive politically and economically, though still an adversarial threat to be dealt with.[6] This is evident in the expansion of the carceral state and the normalization of a police and criminal legal apparatus that exists largely "to ensure that those who have fallen don't create further disturbances, and to haul them away to prison if they do."[7] Human devaluation in the age of neoliberalism has put even active resistance movements on the defensive, compelling progressive activists today to stake their work on the question of whether or not Black lives even matter. In this moment, one might be tempted to return in spirit to the heady days of civil rights era liberalism, in order to bring back a more formal commitment to competition and to restore the dignity of competitor status. But such a move would do little to challenge the workings of a society set up to reproduce, and to routinize and normalize, a relation in which a victor class partitions and stands over the fallen, armed to the teeth. Part of what is needed today is a more critical dialogue about the ideological girders of a society set up to produce winners and losers. "Let us be dissatisfied," as King might have said.[8] In this final chapter, I offer some parting remarks on the legacy of Du Bois's critique of the competitive society by way of a brief comparison with King's mature reflections on the ideologies of competitive liberalism.

"'Cooperative Competition' / 'Noble Competition'"

At some point in the late 1940s or early 1950s, likely while he was still a seminarian, King drafted a set of notes for a prospective sermon on the idea of a more "cooperative" form of competition. The piece never made its way to the pulpit, at least not in the form in which it was initially conceived. But the draft is significant in that it reveals a young King wrestling with the terms of the competitive society, reflecting on whether or not a competitive way of life could be squared with Christian moral teachings. "Many would affirm that men reach their highest level of productivity under competitive conditions," he began. "Our whole economic structure is built upon it." King pointed out that Jesus knew of the temptations of the competitive form, the "power that competition held over men." But Jesus indicated a more "noble" way to embrace the "conception of competition" and "rescue it from many of its dangers." In a passage that plainly anticipates the conclusion to one of his most legendary sermons, King ended this earlier draft by suggesting, "If you must use the power of competition; if you must compete with one another; . . . Compete with one another in humility. See [who] can be the truest servant."[9]

The legendary version came many years later, on February 4, 1968, precisely two months before King was killed in Memphis while battling in solidarity with the poor and just weeks after he delivered his tribute to Du Bois at Carnegie Hall. In front of his own congregation at Ebenezer Baptist Church in Atlanta, King spoke of a "drum major instinct," a basic drive to get out front, to get the better of others, to shine in the glory of competitive triumph. In this latter version, King makes a much stronger claim about human nature, although it is worth pointing out that the strongest passages to this effect, including the very idea of an inherent "drum major instinct or impulse," reflect King's adaptation of a 1952 homily, "Drum-Major Instincts," written by a White liberal, the Methodist preacher J. Wallace Hamilton.[10]

What King described in the earlier draft as an idea about how to boost economic productivity, a "conception of competition" that had been made to
rationalize modern capitalism, is presented in the latter version as an inexorable feature of human behavior in its natural state. To be sure, in "The
Drum Major Instinct," King would go on to point out, in his own original
terms, that the competitive ethic had been mobilized for partisan political
purposes, explicitly as a means of fomenting racial divisiveness within the
ranks of the working class. "The poor white has been put into this position,"
King says, "where through blindness and prejudice, he is forced to support
his oppressors" and where "the only thing he has going for him is the false
feeling that he's superior because his skin is white." And of course King concludes with a series of claims prefaced by a conditional clause: "If you want
to say that I was a drum major, say that I was a drum major for justice. Say
that I was a drum major for peace. I was a drum major for righteousness."[11]

One implication of the conditional construction, which appears in both
sermons, is that for King we face a choice, or perhaps several possible
choices, in our embrace of the competitive society. Preaching to a bourgeois
Christian audience at Ebenezer in 1968, playing to middle-class values and
ahistorical presumptions about a fallen humanity, King seems to have pursued a moderate tack befitting of the scene, suggesting that if we embrace
the competitive way of life, as bourgeois liberals might, then we can at least
try to do so more or less ethically. This reading is consistent with what Cornel West has described as a "sanitized" appropriation of King's most popular works.[12] But surely we can find the rudiments of a more radical stance in
these sermons and in other speeches and writings of the period as well as
something closer to a Du Boisian critique of White world ideology. Again,
the conditional: "If you must use the power of competition; if you must
compete with one another." A more plausible reading would conclude that
under certain conditions we find ourselves backed into the "use" of competition, that the "conception of competition" is not simply a categorical
representation of a universal human drive but also a manufactured idea or
rationale that we ought to question and challenge, especially in its role as
an ideological crutch for "our whole economic structure."

This latter reading is consistent with King's mature disillusionment with
the liberal paradigm. During the last years of his life, King grew increasingly frustrated with the civil rights emphasis on legal protection of equal
opportunity. "Public accommodations did not cost the nation anything; the

right to vote did not cost the nation anything," he said to a Howard University audience in 1966. In order really to confront the gulf "between the privileged and the underprivileged, . . . in order to solve this problem, not only will it mean the restructuring of the architecture of American society but it will cost the nation something."[13] And just as Du Bois had argued in 1933 that "there is something radically wrong with an industrial system that turns out simultaneously paupers and millionaires and sets the world starving because it has too much food," the mature King sought to vivify the cruel irony of "islands of poverty in a vast sea of prosperity," to invoke one of his more memorable and frequently iterated phrases.[14] "No one can overlook the wonders that science has wrought for our lives," he said, echoing Du Bois's account of the expansion of social and productive capacity under modern capitalism. But "the question on the agenda must read: why should there be hunger and privation in any land, in any city, at any table, when man has the resources and the scientific know-how to provide all mankind with the basic necessities of life?"[15] King's insistence on a redistribution that would cost something, that would genuinely cut into the material basis of White privilege, along with his curiosity about the factors that forestall such a development, open a window onto a critique of liberal ideology, including a concern about a stubborn vision, what he would describe essentially as an archaic architectural rendering of a society set up to facilitate private competition.

For King and Du Bois, the "conception of competition" had come to reflect an outmoded way of thinking, an ideological crutch of White world privilege that far too many subscribe to and far too dogmatically. There may be occasions for which iron can be made to sharpen iron, as if public servants could be made to compete over selflessness. But when it comes to how we approach questions of basic human need and social interaction, "the contemporary tendency in our society," King says, "is to base our distribution on scarcity, which has vanished, and to compress our abundance into the overfed mouths of the middle and upper classes until they gag with superfluity." We are "clinging to archaic thinking." We desperately need to expose and negate "the outmoded assumptions of the scarcity society" and its "deeply ingrained individualism."[16] And such archaic *thinking*— the presupposition of competitive battles among private individuals, the presupposition of unequal outcomes, of the sheer inevitability of a society composed of winners and losers—is a conceptual reproduction of an underlying competitive *form* that is equally obsolete. Though King was never comfortable with a materialist analysis in the traditional Marxist sense, he came to see that material conditions induce competitive behavior and that a logic of capital accumulation "encourages a cutthroat competition and selfish ambition that inspire men to be more I-centered than thou-centered."[17] There would be no adequate challenge to selfishly competitive social relations without a challenge to the logic of capital accumulation and its institutionalization.

In 1967, referring explicitly to the legacy of Du Bois, King insisted that "racism is still the hound of hell which dogs the tracks of our civilization."[18] Throughout his life, King drew inspiration from Du Bois's sense that European modernity had brought to bear a set of ideas and practices that could not be sustained and that the "dark world," what King occasionally referred to as the "colored world," stood poised to "inject new meaning into the veins of Western Civilization."[19] King sought to sharpen and empower a Black radical criticism that could expose and sharpen contradictions within modern society. At issue, at least in part, was a European civilization, a White world, that had erected a common sense on the supposition of scarcity and the need to compete over resources, a presumption that the poor will in effect always be with us and that we cannot avoid a world partitioned between winners and losers. Early modern Europeans had been moved to assign a kind of primordial status to conditions of scarcity and thus to the competitive relationships that a rights-based liberalism was founded on. Savvy capitalists had used the "conception of competition" as a means to boost productivity. But for King as for Du Bois, we confront a society now that has outgrown its beliefs and stubbornly clings to ideologies and rhetorics of competition and competitiveness in ways that help to ensure that material redistribution will not come to pass, that privilege will not have to endure significant cost and that there will be no "restructuring of the architecture of American society."

"The Regrettable Conclusion"

The evidence marshaled in this book may not be enough to support a general claim about a twentieth-century intellectual tradition, but even a cursory review of King's mature critical theory shows that Du Bois's suspicions of competitive liberalism were made to animate and sustain a critical legacy that outlived their Depression era genesis. My sense, of course, is that this legacy might again be made to inspire a more critical dialogue about a twenty-first-century neoliberal order. Part of what I have sought to convey throughout the book is that the critique of the competitive society is not meant to cash out at the ethical register. The critique itself exposes the limitations of an ethical approach. It is important to emphasize that Du Bois inaugurates a far more radical line of attack, one that sets out to expose how a menu of ethical choices, what are taken to be the range of available ways in which we might commendably engage one another, is always already circumscribed by the competitive form. Though Du Bois has been the primary inspiration, King may well be the more interesting figure with whom to wrestle over these questions about genre or disciplinary boundary, if only because he is often regarded as a political *ethicist* of sorts, one who, owing perhaps to his Christian heritage, tends toward dehistoricizing reflection about timeless moral principles and individual actions and responsibilities.[20] This, of course, is a partial and rather infelicitous caricature of King's significance as a critical and political theorist. But I might exploit the air of ambivalence surrounding King's status as a radical to drive home one final point, namely, that the competitive society contributes to the endurance of an ugly racial politics and, as such, it is ethically irredeemable.

In 1963, in his famous "Letter from a Birmingham Jail," King claimed that he had "almost reached the regrettable conclusion" that the greatest challenge to the Black freedom struggle was not the rabid White supremacist, nor the committed racist, but rather "the white moderate." King intimated that "shallow understanding from people of good will is more frustrating than absolute misunderstanding from people of ill will."[21] In *Dusk of Dawn*, Du Bois said virtually the same thing.[22] He went so far as to suggest that, insofar as he had to live in American society and to navigate the contours of the White world, he was "as bad as they are," as bad, that is, as other practitioners of White liberal sensibility.[23] Part of what disillusionment with liberal thinking entails for the mature Du Bois and King, according to Michael Dawson, is a shift "from hope to despair," particularly as regards "their evaluation of white willingness to 'accept' black equality, the evaluation of the nature of American society, and the assessment of prospects for gaining full democratic citizenship."[24] I would add that what brings Du Bois, if not also King, to the precipice of despair is at least partly a sense that, wittingly or not, we are all conscripts of the competitive society and that, as a more famously pessimistic twentieth-century critic once put it, "wrong life cannot be lived rightly."[25]

Consider a brief anecdote. In 2011, my family and I moved to Atlanta, where I had taken a teaching job at Morehouse College. In our search for housing, we stumbled on a 1920s cottage in Reynoldstown, an eastside Atlanta neighborhood that had been settled by former slaves after the Civil War and that, like many "Intown Atlanta" neighborhoods, was undergoing rapid gentrification. The newer homeowners and renters tended to be educated White professionals. They invariably thought of themselves as people of goodwill, politically conscious and conscientious, progressive in many ways. About a year after my family and I moved in, a nonprofit real-estate developer sought community support to build a five-story, rent-subsidized senior apartment complex on a vacant lot in the heart of the neighborhood. While many in the community thought it was a fine idea, a way to help transition longtime neighborhood residents, including many older women of color, into an affordable assisted-living space, those who owned property adjacent to the would-be development were almost entirely concerted in their opposition. Neighborhood meetings and community message boards were flooded with horror stories about how property values would be decimated overnight and would never recover. Some even trotted out overtly racist narratives about how sweet grandmothers would move into the new apartments only to take in their lawless, drug-dealing grandsons. The fact that prospective residents of the new complex already lived in Reynoldstown, and in many cases owned homes there and had for decades, did not deter variations on the old *there-goes-the-neighborhood* routine. This overt racism was marginal and was met with considerable opposition, to be sure, though there was literally no effort to challenge its more color-blind iteration, what was taken to be a wholly legitimate concern about declining, or at least insufficiently appreciating, property values.

These kinds of dialogues go on in neighborhoods in cities throughout the country. They speak to a contemporary reality in which wealth is so heavily concentrated in the hands of so few, in which so many strands of the social safety net are so frayed and precarious, that the presumption of a kind of general scarcity looms over a felt imperative to protect whatever competitive advantages one can acquire. At the start of this book, I suggested that despite changes to ownership models in the neoliberal age, the institution of private property ownership, and the general discourse surrounding our legitimate or even natural or inalienable right to what belongs to us and not to others, remains perhaps the principal institutional and discursive mechanism though which society's winners declare victory over the losers. It has been said that "in the end everything comes down to competition, so long as private property exists," because "private property isolates everyone in his own crude solitariness," and because everyone "has the same interest as his neighbor, one landowner stands antagonistically confronted by another, one capitalist by another, one worker by another."[26] It has also been said that "as long as white men can be taught to believe that the presence of black men threatens their means of existence, so long will their general attitude be one of enmity," and as long as "the fallacy of economic fear survives, so long will economic competition create race prejudice."[27] In the case of one community dialogue over a rent-subsidized senior residence, it was quite clear that White moderate homeowners found themselves compelled to treat their principal investment as, well, an investment, as private capital. They were driven to fend off would-be threats to the accumulation of its exchange value, irrespective of what such behavior might entail for those who are unable to compete. And the endurance of a racialist logic, hidden or secreted away by race-neutral ideologies of the competitive form, manifested itself yet again as a necessary background condition for the reproduction and legitimation of unequal outcomes, winners and losers.

This anecdote is meant to emphasize the ways in which even avowed liberals, King's "people of good will," find themselves compelled to assume a competitive posture toward others. Even if we set out to resist the entrepreneurial turn, even if we shun the pressures to market ourselves in everything that we do, to court private investment in currencies old and new, dollars and "likes," it is almost impossible to resist the logic of competition in what is perceived to be a struggle for survival, a purportedly rational and eminently responsible quest for financial security in a precarious economy. In my all-too-mundane Reynoldstown example, what most residents recognized as a real problem—a situation in which longtime neighborhood residents, mostly older women of color, were being forced out of their homes due to skyrocketing rents or property taxes, or had simply gotten on in their years and were ready to transition into an assisted-living arrangement—was entirely circumscribed by the competitive form. It is this form that undergirds and structures a competitive ethos that is incredibly difficult to resist, even if we are persuaded to try, and that effectively ensures that even the most courageous acts of individual resistance amount to exceptional—and according to the terms of the ideology, exceptionally irrational—instances of self-sacrifice. It is worth noting here that King's lived example of asceticism, which was exceptional even among the most selfless servants of the Black freedom struggle and which put a tremendous strain on his family, is a case in point.

Public life in the United States is held together, in part, by a fetishism of competition and competitiveness. At the level of abstraction, we celebrate individual rights and equal opportunity, while at the level of lived reality, we bear a freedom to do battle with one another, as private individuals and almost always from a position of fear and uncertainty. What has grown into a hypercompetitive culture contributes to the consolidation of what I have described as a compensatory model of democracy, one in which we find ourselves compelled to engage in public life, to engage one another's needs and concerns, only insofar as we can be reasonably confident in a tangible return on our private investment. Although this book has focused on Du Bois's critique of liberalism and capitalism and has not sought to contribute to democratic theory, as so much of the Du Bois studies literature has, I conclude with an appeal to another vision of democracy, to a sense of what gets lost, what possibilities get foreclosed, in the absence of a critique of the competitive form and its sustaining ideologies. It must be said that the critique itself is animated by a more participatory or communal vision, however speculative, of what our shared public life can and ought to be. While Du Bois has been criticized for the theoretical framework that he allows to shape his democratic purview, for his inability to shed a Weberian conception of elite rulership in favor of a more classical model of shared political action, clearly his mature critical theory, his disillusionment with White world liberalism, is moved by the conviction that, as King perhaps more adequately put it, "when an individual is no longer a true participant, when he no longer feels a sense of responsibility to his society, the content of democracy is emptied."[28] My point is simply that in our dogmatic embrace of competition and competitiveness, we run headlong into a web of constraints that forecloses our capacity even to show concern for one another, let alone act on such concerns in a concerted manner. If, as Du Bois once said, "criticism is the soul of democracy and the safeguard of modern society," then, as a mature King implored, "let us be dissatisfied."

NOTES

Chapter 1. A More Perfect Union

1. Madison, "Federalist No. 51," 264.

2. Here it is perhaps worth highlighting the work of Joseph Schumpeter, whose 1942 publication of *Capitalism, Socialism, and Democracy* has had a lasting impact on what we might call the economization of the political, in particular the establishment of competitive market principles as a basis for scholarly understanding of how political life ought to function.

3. These biographical claims, which I introduce only in passing here at the outset, are documented in greater detail throughout the book. The most comprehensive biography of Du Bois is, of course, David Levering Lewis's two-volume Pulitzer Prize–winning study, *W. E. B. Du Bois: Biography of a Race, 1868–1919* and *W. E. B. Du Bois: The Fight for Equality and the American Century, 1919–1963*.

4. Dawson, *Black Visions*, 17–18, 273–280.

5. "It is the strife of all honorable men of the twentieth century," Du Bois said in 1903, "to see that in the future competition of races the survival of the fittest shall mean the triumph of the good, the beautiful, and the true; that we may be able to preserve for future civilization all that is really fine and noble and strong, and not continue to put a premium on greed and impudence and cruelty." Du Bois, *Souls of Black Folk*, 79. See also Du Bois, "Evolution of the Race Problem," 209–224.

6. Du Bois, *Souls of Black Folk*, 19. As for contemporary criticism, consider the example of Domenico Losurdo, who concludes his rich and race-attentive counterhistory of the liberal tradition by pointing out that "liberal thought has vigorously insisted on the need for competition between individuals in the market, in order to develop social wealth and the productive forces." This, he says, is a "major historical merit to be acknowledged." Losurdo's concern has to do principally with "the awful exclusion clauses," the histories and living legacies of formal and informal barriers to equal opportunity. Losurdo, *Liberalism*, 343–344. Or consider Danielle Allen, who worries not only about how Black people historically have suffered loss and defeat but also about how the competitive form as such guarantees loss and defeat. Still, she says, we can best respond to this

predicament by setting out to cultivate a cross-racial commitment to sacrifice, a willingness to take turns winning and losing and to share in both the benefits and the burdens of competitive interactions. Allen, *Talking to Strangers*. Such a suggestion might appear to be consistent with Du Bois's legacy. After all, "we can't all *always* attain the heights." Maybe we can take turns. Such was essentially Schumpeter's point. But Du Bois, for his part, puts these words in the mouth of an imaginary White friend, a figure who stands in as a kind of ideal-typical symbolization of progressive liberal ideals that Du Bois simply cannot abide.

7. "I am not worried about being inconsistent," Du Bois said in 1934. "I do not care what I said in 1910 or 1810 or in BC 700." Du Bois, "Segregation in the North," 1239–1240. Regarding Du Bois's elusiveness, consider the testimony of one critic who describes Du Bois as "preeminently a dialectician," a writer who "frequently championed apparently opposing positions, sometimes within the scope of this single paragraph. Thus he could be a spirited advocate of pan-Africanism, while insisting that African people were members of the world community centered in universal values. He could defend African Americans' institutional separatism, while crusading relentlessly for their citizenship rights. He could propose an open and inclusive American society and still oppose the radical integrationism of Walter White and Thurgood Marshall, who argued that segregation inherently implied inequality.... There was a warfare between [Du Bois's] loyalties as social democrat and racial romantic, another battle between his impulses as traditionalist and iconoclast. There was a tension between his austerity and his enthusiasm, another between his elitism and his folkishness, and yet another between his blatant Prussianism and his latent Bohemianism." Moses, *Afrotopia*, 136, 149. Or, as Kwame Appiah puts it: Du Bois's "path would be scientific and romantic; it would be fact-bound and fanciful, liberal and illiberal, collectivist and individualist. It would be ethnocentric and universal in outlook. It would be the story of his singular self." Appiah, *Lines of Descent*, 6–7; see also 19–20, for discussion of further contradictions in Du Bois's thought. To my mind, this inconsistency has something to do with Du Bois's struggle to combine an idealist's longing with an activist's pragmatism. As Gerald Horne puts it, while "his passion for socialism, peace, and equality remained immutable throughout" his life, "Du Bois was not one to cling to a point of view if he felt that changing times had undermined it." Horne, *Black and Red*, 7–8. For a discussion of Du Bois as an author of "fugitive pieces," as he once characterized the essays that make up *The Souls of Black Folk*, see Balfour, *Democracy's Reconstruction*, 17–19.

8. Du Bois's efforts to work from a position of disillusionment might be said to align with Robyn Marasco's recent account of critical theorization "at the heights of despair." Marasco, *Highway of Despair*, 6.

9. See Bell, "What Is Liberalism?"; Gunnell, "Archeology of American Liberalism"; Gunnell, *Imagining the American Polity*.

10. See Mirowski and Plehwe, *Road from Mont Pèlerin*; Dardot and Laval, *New Way of the World*; Burgin, *Great Persuasion*; Foucault, *Birth of Biopolitics*; Peck, *Constructions of Neoliberal Reason*; William Davies, *Limits of Neoliberalism*.

11. See Harvey, *Brief History of Neoliberalism*; Brown, *Undoing the Demos*; and Mirowski, *Never Let a Serious Crisis Go to Waste*. Harvey, who offers perhaps the most prominent Marxist account of neoliberalism's classical heresies, tends to underscore the ways in which neoliberal practices depart from classical liberal theory. Brown and Mirowski draw more heavily on Foucault's non-Marxist account of the neoliberal contrast with classical liberal theory. As Brown notes, quoting Foucault's famous lectures on neoliberalism from the late 1970s, "Foucault insists [that] neoliberalism is not just the 'reactivation of old economic theories'; it is not 'a cover for . . . generalized state power.' In short, it is not 'Adam Smith revived,' the market society that is 'decoded and denounced in Book I of *Capital.*'" Brown, *Undoing the Demos*, 61. Neoliberalism, Brown says, entails "uncoupling the market economy from the political principle of laissez-faire, and here lies the radicalism of Foucault's scholarly intervention" (61–62). Mirowski, while less sympathetic to Foucault's analysis than is Brown, nevertheless credits Foucault for being the first to show that "clearly, we're not in classical liberalism anymore." Mirowski, *Never Let a Serious Crisis*, 60. And as Mirowski notes elsewhere, "What has led so many commentators astray is the fact that" by the 1950s the neoliberals, or least those who comprise what Mirowski calls the "Neoliberal Thought Collective," stopped using the term, "ceased insisting that a rupture with the doctrines of classical liberalism was called for and began public relations efforts to legitimize the movement on the grounds that neoliberalism was but an extension of classical liberal doctrine going all the way back to Adam Smith." Mirowski, afterword in Mirowski and Plehwe, *Road from Mont Pèlerin*, 427.

12. Smith, *Wealth of Nations Books I–III*, 117.

13. Louis Rougier (1938), cited in Foucault, *Birth of Biopolitics*, 161.

14. Foucault, *Birth of Biopolitics*, 118.

15. William Davies, *Limits of Neoliberalism*, 37. On this point, see also Jones, *Masters of the Universe*. Here it is worth mentioning, too, that as Davies points out, "Neoliberals changed their emphasis on different aspects of competition, gradually relinquishing the priority of formal equality (which, in the USA, also underpinned the Jeffersonian ideal of small-scale producers in a marketplace) and increasingly focusing on contingent inequality of outcome as the critical feature and test of a competitive system." Davies, *Limits of Neoliberalism*, 42. This gradual shift would seem to correspond with Du Bois's evolving disillusionment

with the competitive dimensions of liberal theory. In *The Philadelphia Negro*, Du Bois's 1899 ethnographic study, he pointed out that "the little shop, the small trader, the house industry have given way to the department store, the organized company, and the factory" (24). He went on to add that "today ... the application of large capital to the retail business, the gathering of workmen into factories, the wonderful success of trained talent in catering to the whims and taste of customers almost precludes the effective competition of the small store" (85). I highlight this passage simply to indicate that the early Du Bois appears tacitly to have endorsed the idealized image of small-scale liberal competitiveness; his worry expressed in 1899 appears to have been simply that this ideal had already been killed off by big capital, though perhaps the ideal lives on ideologically, in ways that can and ought to be defended. As we will see, into his more mature writings on liberalism, and perhaps as he becomes aware of what Davies and others have described as the early neoliberal turn toward "different aspects of competition," Du Bois seems to have relinquished any appeal to what classical liberal doctrine had regarded as the leveling virtues of small-scale competition.

16. Brown, *Undoing the Demos*, 61. Dieter Plehwe likewise identifies the distinctiveness of neoliberal theory in its "strong emphasis on the social character of economic relations," and he credits Foucault for having discovered this dimension of the work of the German ordoliberals in the 1930s. Plehwe, introduction to Mirowski and Plehwe, *Road from Mont Pèlerin*, 2.

17. It is worth pointing out that, as early as 1911, Schumpeter, whom some have credited as the first theorist of entrepreneurship, described the ethic of the entrepreneur in terms of "the will to conquer: the impulse to fight, to prove oneself superior to others, to succeed for the sake, not of the fruits of success, but of success itself." Schumpeter, *Theory of Economic Development*, 93. More than a century later, the entrepreneurial will to conquer is roundly celebrated in ever more facets of contemporary life. The entrepreneur Peter Thiel, for example, has argued that the best competitors are those who can dominate any and all would-be players and effectively write the rules of the game. This sentiment has become much more than just business strategy; it is the ethic of those who aspire to "win" at life. Thiel, "Competition Is for Losers."

18. Brown, *Undoing the Demos*, 36.

19. Davies, *Limits of Neoliberalism*, 41. In "The Birth of a New American Aristocracy," a brilliant essay on contemporary inequality and class politics, Matthew Stewart has tapped into this phenomenon in his account of why the "delusion of merit is so hard to shake," for "if the system can be gamed, well then, our ability to game the system has become the new test of merit."

20. Brown, *Undoing the Demos*, 42.

21. Singh, *Black Is a Country*, 89, 60, 87, 60–61. It is worth pointing out that

Singh's analysis of the liberal reformation starts from the presumption that "the 1930s was a watershed decade for the development of *egalitarian* alternatives to classical liberalism" (60–61, emphasis added) and that the Keynesians and New Deal reformers were the driving force. Part of my point in highlighting the emergence of a neoliberal movement during the 1930s is to caution how the usual emphasis on egalitarian reforms obscures our appreciation of the ways in which avowedly liberal reformers also pursued explicitly *inegalitarian* alternatives to classical liberalism.

22. Porter, *Problem of the Future World*, 3, 11. See also Winant, *World Is a Ghetto*.

23. Brown, *Undoing the Demos*, 44.

24. Harvey, *Enigma of Capital*, 28.

25. Cedric J. Robinson, *Black Marxism*, 2.

26. Melamed, "Racial Capitalism," 77.

27. Singh, "On Race, Violence," 30–31. In this essay, which was written more than a decade after *Black Is a Country*, Singh does not engage with Du Bois, though he certainly could have. Singh goes on to note that the theory of racial capitalism "challenges common tendencies within liberal and Marxist intellectual traditions to think of race in terms of ascriptive fixity, and in turn to align racial differentiation with static notions of precapitalist particularity. Instead, it highlights the modern, uniquely fabricated quality of racial distinctions as a domain for the elaboration of a permanent reserve of institutionalized coercion or surplus violent capacity that persistently shadows normative processes of value formation within certain varieties of capitalist society. Race in this view is a typically flexible and fungible mode of ascription that from its inception retains important affinities with criminalization, punishment, and disposability of poor, idle and/or surplus labor" (31). All of this is consistent with Du Bois's mature account of the exploitation of racial ascription within liberal-capitalist societies.

28. Robinson, *Black Marxism*, 2; Singh, "On Race, Violence," 31.

29. See Du Bois, *Black Reconstruction*, 584–585. See also Roediger, *Seizing Freedom*. Consider Stephanie Shaw's argument that Du Bois's analysis of Black labor in *Black Reconstruction* is in fact nothing new for him and that the first chapters of *The Souls of Black Folk*, for example, demonstrate a "systematic examination of postemancipation black labor." Shaw, *W. E. B. Du Bois*, 21.

30. See, for example, Du Bois, "Negro and Social Reconstruction." In the late 1910s and early 1920s, before he had engaged seriously with Marx, Du Bois wrote a series of *Crisis* articles on economic cooperation, some of which advanced claims about the political potential of Black consumer co-ops. See, for example, Du Bois, "Consumers' Co-operation," 114–115. Mark Van Wienen has shown that Du Bois's emphasis on cooperative economics can be traced back to 1911, when

he published the novel *Quest for the Silver Fleece*. See Van Wienen, *American Socialist Triptych*, 134–135, 178–179. As for the contradictions between Marxist theory and Du Bois's position on a consumers' movement in the 1930s, Bill Mullen points out, "Du Bois's conception of a 'consumerist' socialism is strikingly devoid of both the work and workers whose labor enables consumption at all. Its faith in cooperative economics transcribes optimism about the Soviet experiment and self-determination into a volunteerist politics largely more dependent upon cooperation than class struggle." Mullen, *Un-American*, 77. For our purposes, it is worth noting that toward the end of the 1930s, Du Bois began to shift his attention to the role that Black colleges could play in fomenting revolutionary consciousness and action; by the 1940s, as Eric Porter put it, "He now looked not to a consumers' movement but to Negro colleges for a plan of action." Porter, *Problem of the Future World*, 47. Du Bois's mature vision for the Black college is the subject of discussion in chapter 4.

31. Consider, for example, David Harvey's recovery of Marx on the totality of capital as "value in motion," which underscores the significance of political struggles against the circulation of capital beyond traditional class politics, or the resurgence of interest in Marx on "value-form theory." Harvey, *Marx, Capital, and the Madness*; Endnotes Collective, *Endnotes 2*. See also Dawson, "Hidden in Plain Sight"; and Fraser, "Behind Marx's Hidden Abode."

32. Brown, *Undoing the Demos*, 65. See also Mirowski, *Never Let a Serious Crisis*, 58–59.

33. Marx, *Capital*, 1:873.

34. Eley, "Historicizing the Global, Politicizing Capital," 167. Eley goes on to note, "Whether from the standpoint of the 'future' of capitalism or from the standpoint of its 'origins,' the more classical understanding of capitalism and its social formations as being centered around industrial production in manufacturing begins to seem like an incredibly partial and potentially distortive one, a phase to be found overwhelmingly in the West, in ways that presupposed precisely its absence from the rest of the world and lasted for a remarkably brief slice of historical time" (167). For a cogent discussion of how racial politics have been affected by the onset of a post-Fordist economic model, see Dawson and Francis, "Black Politics."

35. Eley, "Historicizing the Global, Politicizing Capital," 168, 172.

36. Mirowski, *Never Let a Serious Crisis*, 60.

37. Here we might do well to recount David Harvey's more straightforward definition of the neoliberal vision, namely, that "human well-being can best be advanced by liberating individual entrepreneurial freedoms and skills within an institutional framework characterized by strong private property rights." Harvey, *Brief History of Neoliberalism*, 2.

38. Du Bois, *Souls of Black Folk*, 8.

39. See Appiah, "Uncompleted Argument"; Appiah, *In My Father's House*, 28–46; Porter, *Problem of the Future World*; and Olson, "W. E. B. Du Bois and the Race Concept." It is worth noting that Appiah, who years ago condemned what he took to be the irredeemable biologism of Du Bois's theorization of race, has admitted more recently that while Du Bois's "romantic notion of a collective and involuntary striving for an ideal doesn't make much sense to us now, if it ever did . . . there is something important in the implication that races matter because membership in a race allows people—compels people—to work together for common purposes." Appiah, *Lines of Descent*, 91.

40. Olson, "W. E. B. Du Bois," 226–227. See also Olson, *Abolition of White Democracy*.

41. Ibid., 219.

42. Du Bois, *Dusk of Dawn*, 141.

43. Geuss, *Philosophy and Real Politics*, 25.

44. Dawson, *Blacks In and Out*, 180. For a commentary on how late capitalism has become "anti-normative," essentially taking itself for granted, ceasing to make its case for how ordinary people might benefit, see Boltanski and Chiapello, *New Spirit of Capitalism*, 35. It is perhaps worth reflecting on Lester Spence's argument "against the neoliberal turn in black politics." Despite the fact that he offers to date one of the only book-length treatments of this crucial topic, Spence is inattentive to political theory and the history of ideas, and he unwittingly endorses the neoliberal naturalization of the competitive form. While Spence is clearly worried about how neoliberal practices signal cycles of loss and defeat for a disproportionate number of Black people, he simply assumes that politics across time and place is and must be about competition. Spence, *Knocking the Hustle*, 8. There is much to admire in Spence's analysis, but his explicit embrace of the competitive form is perhaps an example of the arrested imagination that Dawson worries about. Spence cites the 1930s as a moment in which the "inequality level dropped" because "less powerful groups fought against more powerful groups and won" (8). He marks the late 1970s as the moment of historical emergence for the neoliberal movement and does not consider the ways in which competitive market ideologies not only were not challenged but also were consciously consolidated during and immediately after the Great Depression.

45. For a helpful synthesis of how critics of neoliberal theory and practice have mobilized this broad notion of ideology critique, see Gilbert, "What Kind of Thing Is 'Neoliberalism'?"

46. Kelley, *Freedom Dreams*.

47. Davies, *Limits of Neoliberalism*, 69. Mirowski notes that "neoliberalism as

a worldview has sunk its roots deep into everyday life, almost to the point of passing as the 'ideology of no ideology,'" and Foucault has likewise argued that ideology critique is simply insufficient to an understanding of the pervasiveness of neoliberal rationality. See Mirowski, *Never Let a Serious Crisis*, 28, and Foucault, *Birth of Biopolitics*, 48–49.

48. "The critical mind, if it is to renew itself and be relevant again," Latour says, "is to be found in the cultivation of a stubbornly realist attitude . . . a realism dealing with what I will call matters of concern, not matters of fact. The mistake we made, the mistake I made, was to believe that there was no efficient way to criticize matters of fact except by moving away from them and directing one's attention toward the conditions that made them possible. But this meant accepting much too uncritically what matters of fact were. . . . Reality is not defined by matters of fact. Matters of fact are not all that is given in experience. Matters of fact are only very partial and, I would argue, very polemical, very political renderings of matters of concern and only a subset of what could also be called states of affairs. It is this second empiricism, this return to the realist attitude, that I'd like to offer as the next task for the critically minded." Latour, "Why Has Critique Run Out of Steam?" 231–232.

49. Michael Dawson has argued that a "second period" of Black radicalism in the twentieth century, the Black Power era, which has had an effect on the interpretation of Du Bois, was affected by a "more diffuse theoretical understanding of what constituted Marxism" (*Blacks In and Out*, 122). The "emphasis on Maoism" and the idea "that knowledge came from the people and even more so from practice (practical work) meant a shift in many black circles away from works such as Marx's *Capital* to Lenin's *What Is to Be Done*. . . . While there were still some theoretical debates, such as over the status of blacks within the United States (usually under the rubric of the 'national question'), there was much less theoretical focus in the second period than in the first" (123).

50. There are, of course, many secondary accounts of Du Bois's alleged Marxism. In addition to Horne, *Black and Red*, and Van Wienen, *American Socialist Triptych*, the most helpful book-length studies include Mullen, *Un-American*; Kate A. Baldwin, *Beyond the Color Line*; Reed, *Fabianism and the Color Line*; and Marable, *W. E. B. Du Bois*.

51. Singh, *Black Is a Country*, 74.

52. Porter, *Problem of the Future World*, 58.

53. See Du Bois, "My Evolving Program," 56.

54. Chandler, *X*, 31. Chandler goes on to note that, in the tradition of Du Bois but also C. L. R. James, Cedric Robinson, and Fred Moten, we might think of "Black studies [as] the critique of western civilization" (174).

55. Glaude, *Democracy in Black*.

56. Harding, "Toward the Black University," 157.

57. Michael Dawson identifies the later Du Bois and the later King as the two exemplary "disillusioned liberals" in the African American political theoretical tradition. See Dawson, *Black Visions*, 17–18, 273–280.

58. Fred Moten, quoted in McCarthy, "Low End Theory."

59. Streek, *How Will Capitalism End?* 14–15.

Chapter 2. Black Radicalism as Liberal Disillusionment

1. Du Bois, *Dusk of Dawn*, 78.

2. See Du Bois, "Conservation of the Races."

3. See Holloway, *Confronting the Veil*; Gilmore, *Defying Dixie*; Eben Miller, *Born along the Color Line*; Lewis, *W.E.B. Du Bois: The Fight*; Singh, *Black Is a Country*.

4. For a more detailed account, including discussion of Du Bois's contributions, see Cedric J. Robinson, *Black Marxism*; Kelley, *Freedom Dreams*; and Bogues, *Empire of Liberty*. To my mind, C. L. R. James's *The Black Jacobins* remains the classic account of the Black radical critique of European liberalism. For more on the racist underpinnings of the liberal tradition, see Mehta, *Liberalism and Empire*; Sala-Molins, *Dark Side of the Light*; Losurdo, *Liberalism*, and the work of Charles W. Mills, notably, "Racial Liberalism."

5. Kelley, *Freedom Dreams*.

6. Du Bois, "Study of the Negro Problems," 7.

7. Dawson, *Black Visions*, 13, 244.

8. See Bell, "What Is Liberalism?" See also Gunnell, "Archeology of American Liberalism" and *Imagining the American Polity*.

9. Du Bois, *Darkwater*, 66.

10. Bell, "What Is Liberalism?" 692, 698–699.

11. Sabine, *History of Political Theory*, 620. Du Bois's pre-1930 use of the term *laissez-faire* seems to appear most notably, if not exclusively, in *The Suppression of the African Slave-Trade* (1896). In that text, it is not clear that Du Bois is critical of the philosophy, which he seems to associate with the economic motives behind the abolition of enslavement.

12. Du Bois, *Dusk of Dawn*, 137. One is reminded of David Brion Davis's observation that "John Locke, the great enemy of all absolute and arbitrary power, was the last major philosopher to seek a justification for absolute and perpetual slavery." Davis, *Problem of Slavery*, 45.

13. See Singh, *Black Is a Country*, 60–61, 87. See also Ira Katznelson's prefatory remarks on Du Bois's reaction to the New Deal in Katznelson, *When Affirmative Action Was White*, and Porter, *Problem of the Future World*, 32–33.

14. Du Bois, *Dusk of Dawn*, 82.

15. Singh, *Black Is a Country*, 82, 91.

16. Du Bois to Abram L. Harris, January 6, 1933, Du Bois Papers. Harris responded: "A good Marxian ought to know the intellectual and social background of Marx's work. This I should think is best gotten from any of the standard works on economic doctrine and the history of political thought. I would suggest your browsing through Gide and Rist, *History of Economic Doctrines*; Halevy, *The Growth of Philosophic Radicalism*; and Dunning, *Political Thought from Rousseau to Spencer*. The following by Marx and Engels should be read: Marx, "Gotha Program," "Wage Labor and Capital," and "Value, Price, and Profit" (in *The Essentials of Marx*, Algernon Lee, Vanguard Press); *The Critique of Political Economy* (if *Capital* has not been read); and Engels, *Feuerbach and the Roots of the Socialist Philosophy: Socialism from Utopia to Science*; and *Landmarks of Scientific Socialism*. After you finish these I suggest that you look into Marx's *Revolution and Counter-Revolution* and *The 18th Brumaire of Louis Bonaparte*." Harris to Du Bois, January 7, 1933, Du Bois Papers.

17. Du Bois to Harris, January 27, 1931, Du Bois Papers.

18. Harris, "Future Plan and Program."

19. Locke, *Two Treatises of Government*, 350.

20. Holloway, *Confronting the Veil*, 95.

21. Du Bois, *Darkwater*, 42.

22. Holloway, *Confronting the Veil*, 96. See also Boustan, *Competition in the Promised Land*.

23. Marx and Engels, *Communist Manifesto*, 219.

24. Holloway, *Confronting the Veil*, 103. It is worth mentioning that a positive emphasis on the need for racial unity within the working class, rather than Du Bois's more diagnostic emphasis on the factors that delimit this possibility, seems to have been the standard line among the younger generation Howard University intellectuals. Ralph Bunche would remark in 1935 that "if there is any ideology which offers any hope to the Negro it would seem to be that which identifies his interests with the white workers of the nation," and E. Franklin Frazier, in the same year, would note that "there are signs that the question of the status of the Negro is losing its purely racial character and becoming tied up with the struggle of white and black workers against the white landlords and capitalists" (both Bunche and Frazier quoted in Singh, *Black Is a Country*, 71). Singh goes on to mention the 1935 gathering of intellectuals and activists at the Joint Committee on National Recovery, which sought to explore the racial implications of the New Deal; Singh points out that "Frazier, Bunche, [A. Philip Randolph] ... as well as Socialist Party Chairman Norman Thomas, Communist vice presidential candidate James Ford, and the Trotskyist Workers' Party representative, Ernest Rice McKinney," that is, "every speaker, *with the exception of Du Bois*," underscored an

emphasis on the promise of racial solidarity within the ranks of labor (81). My point is simply that Du Bois was distinctive in his driving focus on the sources and enduring power of racial competition and divisiveness.

25. This is, of course, a complicated matter in the context of Du Bois's evolving thinking about revolutionary politics and his shifting appropriations of Marxist categories of analysis. It could be argued that however seriously he began to engage with Marx in the mid-1930s, Du Bois never strayed too far from the position he laid out in a 1921 *Crisis* editorial on class struggle: "Theoretically we are part of the world proletariat in the sense that we are mainly an exploited class of cheap laborers; but practically we are not a part of the white proletariat and are not recognized by that proletariat to any great extent. We are the victims of their physical oppression, social ostracism, economic exclusion and personal hatred; and when in self-defense we seek sheer subsistence we are howled as scabs." Du Bois, "Class Struggle," 555. Bill Mullen has recently developed what could be seen as another line of analysis on this point. Mullen argues that in *Black Reconstruction*, in Du Bois's famous if controversial account of a "General Strike" put on by Black slaves during the Civil War, Du Bois envisioned precisely a multiracial proletarian revolution in the United States, in this case one led by Black workers but supported crucially by White workers. See Mullen, *Un-American*, 82–82. I would suggest that this possibility is seen by Du Bois, at least at a particular moment in history and at a particular moment in the plotline in *Black Reconstruction*, as just that, a possibility. Ultimately this is cast by Du Bois as an opportunity missed, a revolutionary moment quashed by what he would describe as the "counter-revolution of property." My point is simply that in the mid-1930s, Du Bois was far more confident in the endurance of a divisive competitive liberalism than he was in the coming of a multiracial proletarian revolution in the classical Marxist sense of the term. This point will be further complicated by a discussion in chapter 4 of what I call the speculative dimension of Du Bois's critical theory.

26. Harris, "Reconstruction and the Negro," 209. These concerns about Du Bois were long standing. See Harris's 1925 letter to V. F. Calverton: "One of these days, I shall lose my objectivity and become a perennial whiner over the race question like my friend Herr Doctor Du Bois, the sentimental lyricist, the master militant-phrase-monger whose caustic tongue is so much given to the utterance of bellicosity that his poor little neurological system suffers paralysis when he attempts to loosen himself from racial subjectivism." "Man you must not attempt to compare me with Du Bois, Johnson, Locke, Miller, et al. . . . In view of the fact that I pay lip-service, which I despise to my heart, to W. E. B. Du Bois and the rest of his sentimental ilk, I suppose the damn habit of thinking them really great is slowly crystalizing." Harris to Calverton, April 6, 1925, Calverton Papers.

27. Du Bois, "My Evolving Program," 56.

28. See Du Bois, *Dusk of Dawn*, 2–3.

29. Du Bois, "Conservation of the Races," 819.

30. See Du Bois, *Dusk of Dawn*, 2–3. It is this concern that would allow Du Bois to say, in an important address in 1938 at Fisk University, "Democracy does not and cannot mean freedom. On the contrary it means coercion. It means submission of the individual will to the general will and it is justified in this compulsion only if the will is general and not the will of special privilege." Du Bois, "Revelation of Saint Orgne the Damned," 120.

31. Du Bois, *Dusk of Dawn*, 14. Underscoring both a sense of disillusionment with liberal political objectives and a subsequent turn toward a focus on the economic workings of twentieth-century society, Du Bois would go on to say that "a continued agitation which had for its object simply free entrance into the present economy of the world, that looked at political rights as an end in itself rather than as a method of reorganizing the state, and that expected through civil rights and legal judgments to re-establish freedom on a broader and firmer basis, was not so much wrong as short-sighted; that the democracy which we had been asking for in political life must sooner or later replace the tyranny which now dominated industrial life."

32. See Marx and Engels, *German Ideology*, 67.

33. See Du Bois, "My Evolving Program," where Du Bois associates the turn to Marx with his "post-1928 strategy." Elsewhere Du Bois indicates that a real shift in his thinking occurs in the wake of a 1933 address at Fisk University: "To me it [the address at Fisk] was the beginning of a new line of thought. . . . From that day I began to read and study Karl Marx. I began to understand my recent visit to Russia. I became interested in the New Deal and I wanted to supplement the liberalism of Charles Sumner with the new economic contribution of the 20th century." Du Bois, "Field and Function," 102. In the next chapter, I consider Du Bois's engagement with Marx, but it is worth noting here that in the summer of 1933, Du Bois returned to Atlanta University to lead a graduate seminar on "Karl Marx and the Negro." Marx's *German Ideology* was not published until 1932 and was not translated into English until 1938, and surviving drafts of the syllabi for Du Bois's courses indicate only that he had engaged with *Capital* and *The Poverty of Philosophy*. It is fair to presume that Du Bois was never a conscious practitioner of what has come to be known, largely in the wake of the early Frankfurt School, as *Ideologiekritik*. For our purposes, this may be a good thing; in recent decades the coherence of a more comprehensive theory of ideology has been subject to compelling scrutiny. See Rosen, *On Voluntary Servitude*; Rosen, "*On Voluntary Servitude* and the Theory of Ideology"; and Geuss, *Idea of a Critical Theory*.

34. Harris and Spero, *Black Worker*, 462–463.

35. Nahum Dimitri Chandler points out that readers rarely pay attention to the sentence *after* the famous line about the "problem of the 20th century as the problem of the color line." Du Bois goes on to identify a "*phase* of this problem that caused the Civil War," which would suggest that, for Du Bois, the problem is not stable or unchanging and that its problematic character courses through different historical phases. The Depression, and the prefiguring of a color-blind liberalism in the years to follow, represents perhaps another phase, one that calls not for an antidiscrimination framework but a critical appraisal of an underlying political-economic form. See Chandler, *X*, 72.

36. Reed, "The 'Color Line' Then and Now," 258. On the historical periods of "race thinking," Reed adds that "although the race idea began to take coherent shape as a metric of hierarchy by the eighteenth century, in the ways we currently presume to understand it, both substantively and evocatively, race became fully delineated within a more general pool of discourses of ascriptive differentiation only in the middle to late nineteenth century."

37. See Harris, "Reconstruction and the Negro" and Harris to Calverton, April 6, 1925.

38. Geuss, *Philosophy and Real Politics*, 25.

39. Du Bois, "Vacation Unique," 224–225. Zamir notes that this text, written in 1889 when Du Bois was still a graduate student at Harvard University, is "an extensive critique and satire of Teutonism (*Anglo-Saxon* and *Teuton* are interchangeable terms for Du Bois), and this at a time when theories about the Teutonic origins of the United States still had widespread currency." Zamir, *Dark Voices*, 49.

40. See, for example, Du Bois, "Segregation in the North" (1934) and "A Negro Nation within the Nation" (1935).

41. Appiah, *Lines of Descent*, 91. Appiah also notes that "Du Bois's account here of racial or national membership is focused on the ideas—or, as we might also say, the principles—expressed in the collective life of a people; and in insisting on this, he is thinking about national history in the ways that would have been familiar to him. It was, after all, the standard understanding of Hegel's philosophy of history: that human experience was the working out of an idea—in fact of something called *the* idea—in history. In the less metaphysical version of the story, which Du Bois borrows not from philosophers but from historians, nations are the historical expressions not of one grand universal Idea but of slightly less grand particular ideas" (89).

42. Du Bois, *Dusk of Dawn*, 69–70.

43. Appiah, *Lines of Descent*, 113.

44. Du Bois, "Conservation of the Races," 819–820.

45. Chandler, *X*, 34.

46. C. L. R. James, "African Independence and the Myth of African Inferiority," 34.

47. Dawson, *Black Visions*, 275.

48. Lewis, *W. E. B. Du Bois: Biography*, 373–374, emphasis added.

Chapter 3. The Ideologies of Racial Capitalism

1. Du Bois, "Where Do We Go from Here?" 154, 159 (often referred to as the Rosenwald Conference lecture).

2. See Du Bois, "Field and Function," 102.

3. See Du Bois, "Karl Marx and the Negro Problem Assignments."

4. See Du Bois, "Letter to Matthew V. Boutte," 304.

5. Du Bois, "My Evolving Program," 69. Du Bois's explicit references to Marx so often express only a basic embrace of a materialist methodological approach, a sort of weak economic determinism. Consider as an example a passage from Du Bois's *Black Reconstruction*: "To the student of government who fastens his attention chiefly on politics, the years 1866 to 1876 were years when the power of the national government remained exclusively democratic, with ultimate control in the hands of the mass of citizens who had the right to vote. But the student who realizes that human activity is chiefly exercised in earning a living and, thus, particularly in the present industrial income—this student will see that the Civil War brought anarchy in the basic economic activities which were gradually hammered and forced into a new and vast monarchy of tremendous power and almost miraculous accomplishment" (584–585). Du Bois would go on to emphasize, in a discussion of the liberal abolitionist Charles Sumner, that "what liberalism did not understand was that" genuine revolutionary change "was economic and involved force. . . . Charles Sumner did not realize, and that other Charles—Karl Marx—had not yet published *Das Kapital* to prove to men that economic power underlies politics" (591). Much has been made of Du Bois's work on "primitive accumulation" and the role of African slavery in the making of the world capitalist system, in particular how *Black Reconstruction* prefigures Eric Williams's important contributions a decade later, in *Capitalism and Slavery*. See Eric Williams, *Capitalism and Slavery* and Taylor, "W. E. B. Du Bois." This matter of "primitive accumulation" will be taken up in greater detail later in the chapter.

6. Cedric J. Robinson, *Black Marxism*, 229.

7. See Gorman, "W. E. B. Du Bois and His Work."

8. See Lewis, *W. E. B. Du Bois: The Fight*, 310, in reference to Du Bois's 1930s correspondence with Abram Harris, the Howard University economics professor

and avowed Marxist theoretician whose work was discussed in some detail in chapter 2, and Singh, *Black Is a Country*, 79–80, in reference to how "Du Bois's forays into economic theory and socialist politics after Amenia were harshly dismissed" by E. Franklin Frazier, Ralph Bunche, and Abram Harris. See also Sidney Hook's works, notably *Towards the Understanding of Karl Marx*, first published in 1933. More recent work on the later Du Bois reinforces a sense of, as Bill Mullen puts it, "Du Bois's staggered and incomplete understandings of Marxism" (*Un-American*, 11). Mullen notes elsewhere that Du Bois offers a "textual overlay of Marxian categories" (57) onto analyses, such as *Black Reconstruction*, that are otherwise uninformed by Marxist theory and that in his more positive vision of socialism, for example, in his account of "consumerist socialism" or "economic cooperatives" during the 1930s, Du Bois "totally abandoned Marxist categories such as surplus value, labor exploitation, and . . . Marx's argument that 'white workers may not be free while wherein the Black is branded'" (74). Mullen's remarkable study, very explicit in its sympathies with Marxist thought and anticapitalist revolutionary politics, offers to date the most thorough account of Du Bois's engagement with Marxism, although Mullen's work is more historical than theoretical, and it focuses primarily on Marx's influence on Du Bois's evolving thinking about political strategy rather than on his critique of the structural workings of capitalist society.

9. Robinson, *Black Marxism*, 2.

10. Dawson, "Hidden in Plain Sight," 147. See also Fraser, "Behind Marx's Hidden Abode" and "Expropriation and Exploitation."

11. See, for example, the essays written in honor of Cedric Robinson in *Futures of Black Radicalism*, edited by Gaye Theresa Johnson and Alex Lubin, and *Race, Capitalism, Justice*, edited by Walter Johnson and Robin D. G. Kelley. See also Clarno, *Neoliberal Apartheid*; Singh, *Race and America's Long War*; and Douglas, "Diagnosing Racial Capitalism."

12. In addition to Cedric Robinson's extended discussion of Du Bois in *Black Marxism*, see Walter Johnson, "To Remake the World."

13. Du Bois's body of work could be said to contribute to either of two schools of Marxist thought that explicitly heed the category of the political. One is the tradition of the so-called autonomist Marxists, who underscore the revolutionary self-activity of various labor groups, including many unwaged workers, those who are often situated outside the traditional category of the industrial proletariat. Here it is worth noting one text in particular, Cleaver's *Reading Capital Politically*, which argues that *Capital* is best understood as an intellectual weapon to be taken up and deployed in a broadly anticapitalist struggle and includes an extended discussion of Du Bois's midcentury Black radical contemporary, C. L. R. James. The autonomist Marxists tend to focus on the nature of

class-consciousness and the development of group solidarities, which are areas in which Du Bois offered significant contributions; the focus of the present chapter, however, lies with the theory and logic of capitalism's social form. The other tradition worth mentioning derives from the recent work of Robert Brenner, Ellen Meiksins Wood, Charles Post, and others—the school of so-called political Marxism. Much of this work has been built around the idea that the emergence of capitalism and a distinctive value-form does not reflect simply the liberation of historical obstacles to human interaction but is, rather, a compulsory order imposed politically. Setting aside concerns about whether or not the "political Marxists" work from a fair reading of Marx, we can point to affinities with Du Bois's insinuation that the presumed "opening" of the competitive society, the idea that capitalism is simply a historical liberation of competitive human nature, obscures the ways in which a regulative social form is imposed and sustained by the beneficiaries of White world orthodoxy. For more on this tradition, see Brenner, *Merchants and Revolution*; Wood, *Origin of Capitalism*; Post, *American Road to Capitalism*; and for a valuable theoretical rebuttal, Davidson, "Is There Anything to Defend in Political Marxism?"

14. See Marable, *W. E. B Du Bois*, and Nembhard, "Cooperative Ownership in the Struggle."

15. Du Bois, "Where Do We Go from Here?" 163. Here it may be worth citing the fuller passage at length: "I propose as the next step which the American Negro can give to the world a new and unique gift. We have tried song and laughter and with rare good humor a bit condescending the world has received it; we have given the world work, hard, backbreaking labor and the world has let black John Henry die breaking his heart to beat the machine. It is now our business to give the world an example of intelligent cooperation, so that when the new industrial Commonwealth comes, we can go into it as experienced people and not again be left on the outside as mere beggars" (162–163).

16. See Adams, *Epic of America*. Although he does not mention Adams explicitly, surely Du Bois was mindful of Adams and likely saw himself working in critical tension with the New England historian, who in 1934 published his own study of the Reconstruction era, a study that, in the words of Herbert Aptheker, conformed to contemporary standards of White racist historiography in its "pro-Bourbon racist bias" and implicit approval of Klan terrorism. See Du Bois, *Correspondence of W. E. B. Du Bois*, 11, and Adams, *America's Tragedy*.

17. Du Bois, *Black Reconstruction*, 182–183. Elsewhere Du Bois describes it as the "American assumption of equal economic opportunity for all, which persisted in the face of facts" (585).

18. Du Bois, *Black Reconstruction*, 183.

19. See "On the Wings of Atalanta," in Du Bois, *Souls of Black Folk*, 54–62.

20. See Marx, "Eighteenth Brumaire of Louis Bonaparte."

21. Du Bois, *Black Reconstruction*, 30; Du Bois, *Dusk of Dawn*, 70.

22. Marx, *Capital*, 179, 229–230, 280.

23. For a recent example of such turf wars, see Patrick Anderson, "Pan-Africanism and Economic Nationalism." Anderson is concerned about labels and the implications of reading Du Bois as a "disciple" of Marxism rather than as an original theorist of and adherent to Pan-Africanism. Although I am sympathetic to Anderson's concern, for reasons that will become clearer as I move into a discussion of the Black college in chapter 4, I would argue that Marx's critique of political economy, his theorization of the totality of capitalist society, the capitalist value-form, and the reproduction of unequal social relations, none of which Anderson addresses in his account of the reductionist class politics of "dogmatic Marxism," provides important theoretical resources that can and should be put into productive conversation with Du Bois's more expansive critical theory of racial capitalism.

24. Du Bois, *Black Reconstruction*, 634–635.

25. Marx, *Capital*, 230, 252.

26. Marx, *Grundrisse*, 552.

27. See also Marx, *Capital*, 433. It is perhaps worth quoting Marx at some length here: "While it is not our intention here to consider the way in which the immanent laws of capitalist production manifest themselves in the external movement of the individual capitals, assert themselves as the coercive laws of competition, and therefore enter into the consciousness of the individual capitalist as the motives which drive him forward, this much is clear: a scientific analysis of competition is possible only if we can grasp the inner nature of capital, just as the apparent motions of heavenly bodies are intelligible to someone who is acquainted with their real motions, which are not perceptible to the senses." Again, Marx does not elaborate on this point ("not our intention here," he says), but the point seems to be that "the inner nature of capital" itself both produces and reinforces competitive behavior. For a helpful discussion of this passage, as well as the passage from the *Grundrisse*, cited above, see Harvey, *Companion to Marx's "Capital,"* 1:166–168, and Harvey, *Enigma of Capital*, 43–47.

28. In a crucial passage from his 1933 address to alumni at Fisk University, Du Bois says, "We discovered widely in the 18th century and the 19th the *use of capital* and it was a great and beneficent discovery; it was the rule of sacrificing present wealth for greater wealth to come." Du Bois, "Field and Function," 111, emphasis mine. The "use of capital" seems to refer again to the popular embrace of an economic system, the way in which a people—or at least the dominant group and its nation-state—employs the mode of production.

29. Lewis, *W. E. B. Du Bois: The Fight*, 10.

30. Du Bois, "Field and Function," 98.

31. Du Bois, *Darkwater*, 16.

32. Marx, *Capital*, 874.

33. See Perelman, *Invention of Capitalism*.

34. Marx, *Capital*, 899.

35. For a nuanced, if concise, account of Marx's complicated views on slavery and wage labor, see Smallwood, "What Slavery Tells Us." Andrew Zimmerman points out that "throughout his long career, Marx emphasized that, while slavery had existed for most of human history, the enslavement of people of African descent in the Americas was a unique and integral component of modern global capitalism. He stated this clearly in *Poverty of Philosophy* (1847), and it remained a theme of constant, growing importance in his subsequent work, from his voluminous writings on the U.S. Civil War through, as Kevin Anderson has recently shown, the three volumes of *Capital*." Zimmerman, "When Liberals Defended Slavery," 87. See Anderson, *Marx at the Margins*. It may be worth noting that in his 1933 course on Marx, Du Bois had his students read two texts: *Capital* and *The Poverty of Philosophy*.

36. Du Bois, *Black Reconstruction*, 5. This passage can be misleading, as the emphasis on production implies that Du Bois's analysis fits seamlessly with Marx's own emphasis on production (at least in *Capital*). Some readers have claimed that Du Bois's opening emphasis on the "Black worker" is something of a contrived attempt by Du Bois to signal an allegiance with Marxist radicalism. Du Bois seems more at home with himself when he refers not to production but to the struggle for income. For a helpful discussion of Du Bois's emphasis on consumer cooperatives and his occasionally strained efforts to square this with the Marxian emphasis on production, see Mullen, *Un-American*, 72–77.

37. Du Bois, *Dusk of Dawn*, 2–3.

38. Du Bois, *World and Africa*, 162. "Not mass production but mass concealment is the sin of the capitalistic system," Du Bois says, for "when the producer is so separated from the consumer in time and space that a mutual knowledge and understanding is impossible, then to regard the industrial process as 'individual enterprise' or the result of 'private initiative' is stupid. It is a social process, and if not socially controlled sinks to anarchy with every possible crime of irresponsible greed."

39. Fraser, "Behind Marx's Hidden Abode," 56–57.

40. Dawson, "Hidden in Plain Sight, 147–148.

41. Melamed, "Racial Capitalism," 78.

42. Cedric J. Robinson, "Oliver Cromwell Cox," 12.

43. For a recent example, see Roediger, *Seizing Freedom*.

44. Douglass, *Narrative of the Life*, 71.

45. Singh, "On Race, Violence," 41, 43.

46. Du Bois, *Darkwater*, 16.

47. Walter Johnson, "To Remake the World," 20.

48. Consider David Theo Goldberg's observation that Justice John Marshall Harlan's dissent in *Plessy v. Ferguson* (1896)—namely, that in effect, "whites will have nothing to fear if the playing field is leveled in the sense of making it possible for all people to compete because whites already have such a leg up and would continue to dominate competitively because of accumulated wealth, education, networks of power, and the like"—coincides with the historic moment when we began to see an appeal to a postracial competitive liberalism, which the later neoliberal project took up more explicitly into the late twentieth century. Goldberg goes on to make the point that what I have called the opening of the competitive society leads to the "privatization of race" or "the undertaking to protect the private expression of *racism* from government intervention. . . . It is really the protection, the privatization, of discrimination, of segregation, of hypersegregation." Goldberg, *Sites of Race*, 27–29.

49. Du Bois, *Darkwater*, 16. It is worth noting, too, that Du Bois would go on to improvise poetically on the color of money, the color of liberal economic freedom, which moves "down through the green waters, on the bottom of the world, where men move to and fro," and then back "up through the foam of green and weltering waters wells this great mass of hatred, in wilder, fiercer violence." And it goes without saying that what Du Bois describes here as "the discovery of personal whiteness" dovetails with his famous reference, in *Black Reconstruction*, to whiteness as "a sort of public and psychological wage." Du Bois, *Black Reconstruction*, 689.

50. Cedric J. Robinson, *Black Marxism*, 204–205. These points are echoed in Oliver Cox's midcentury account of how racism emerged as a necessary ideological crutch of capitalist society. See Robinson, "Oliver Cromwell Cox."

51. Streator, "April 8, 1935, Letter to Du Bois," 90

52. Du Bois, "A Vacation Unique," 224–225.

53. Marx, *Capital*, 169–170; Marx to Engels, June 18, 1862.

54. Du Bois, "Where Do We Go from Here?" 156.

55. Du Bois, "Education and Work," 79.

56. Marx and Engels, *Communist Manifesto*, 220.

57. Du Bois, "Field and Function," 111. It may be worth citing the broader passage at length: "The most distressing fact in the present world is poverty; not absolute poverty, because some folk are rich and many are well to do; not poverty as great as some lands and other historical ages have known; but poverty more poignant and discouraging because it comes after a dream of wealth; of riotous, wasteful, and even vulgar accumulation of individual riches, which suddenly

leaves the majority of mankind today without enough to eat; without proper shelter; without sufficient clothing. We could abolish poverty. Why have we not done this? It is because of greed in the production and distribution of goods and human labor. We discovered widely in the 18th century and the 19th the use of capital and it was a great and beneficent discovery; it was the rule of sacrificing present wealth for greater wealth to come. But instead of distributing this increase of wealth primarily among those who make it we left most workers as poor as possible in order further to increase the wealth of a few. We produced more wealth than the wealthy could consume and yet used this increased wealth to monopolize materials and machines; to buy and sell labor in return for monopoly ownership in the products of labor and for further wealth. We thus not only today produce primarily for the profit of owners and not for use of the mass of people, but we have grown to think that this is the only way in which we can produce."

58. Du Bois, 1942, unknown source, cited in Watkins, "Marxian and Radical Reconstructionist Critique," 126.

59. Du Bois, "Marxism and the Negro Problem." Compare Du Bois's sentiment with that of his Black radical contemporary, C. L. R. James, who wrote in 1947 that "the dialectic teaches that in all forms of society we have known, the increasing development of material wealth brings with it the increasing degradation of the large mass of humanity. Capitalism, being the greatest wealth-producing system so far known, has carried its contradictions to a pitch never known before. Thus it is that the moment when the world system of capitalism has demonstrated the greatest productive powers in history is exactly the period when barbarism threatens to engulf the whole society. The anti-dialecticians stand absolutely dumbfounded before the spectacle of the mastery of nature for human advancement and the degradation of human nature by this very mastery. The greater the means of transport, the less men are allowed to travel. The greater the means of communication, the less men freely interchange ideas. The greater the possibilities of living, the more men live in terror of mass annihilation." James, "Dialectical Materialism," 155.

60. Du Bois, "A Vacation Unique," 224; Marx, *Capital*, 742.

61. Du Bois, "Where Do We Go from Here?" 160. See also Du Bois, "Talented Tenth," 439–440, where, in a reflection on Marx's legacy, Du Bois notes that Marx "declared that the world was not for the few, but for the many; that out of the masses of men could come overwhelming floods of ability and genius, *if we freed men by plan and not by rare chance*," that only then would the world "escape the enduring danger of being run by a selfish few for their own advantage" (emphasis added).

62. Du Bois, "Where Do We Go from Here?" 160.

Chapter 4. The Black College as a Locus of Critique

1. Du Bois, "Where Do We Go from Here?" 159–160.

2. "Honest and earnest criticism," Du Bois said famously in *The Souls of Black Folk*, is the "soul of democracy and the safeguard of modern society," 36.

3. Du Bois, "Conservation of the Races," 819–820.

4. Du Bois, "Education and Work," 106. It is worth noting that these values align neatly with the ethical teachings of what Lynda Morgan has called the "emancipation generation." Indeed, Morgan situates Du Bois within a tradition of postemancipation African American intellectuals who can be said to convey or transmit Black working-class ideas about labor, racism, and freedom, ideas that have their roots in the intellectual production of enslaved women and men. See Morgan, *Known for My Work*.

5. Du Bois, "Negro Nation within the Nation."

6. Du Bois, "Where Do We Go from Here?" 162–163.

7. Joel Olson, "W. E. B. Du Bois," 224.

8. Mullen, *Un-American*, 6. See also Gilroy, *Black Atlantic*.

9. Du Bois, "Revelation of Saint Orgne," 156.

10. Du Bois, "Field and Function," 114, 115.

11. Ibid., 117, 112.

12. Ibid., 129.

13. See Du Bois, *Darkwater*, 47, where, in an essay on the 1917 St. Louis race riots, Du Bois offers the kind of remark that would appear with greater frequency in his writings on higher education in the 1930s and 1940s: "Here, in microcosm, is the sort of economic snarl that arose continually for me and my pupils to solve. We could bring to its unraveling little of the scholarly aloofness and academic calm of most white universities. To us this thing was Life and Hope and Death!"

14. In 1946, Du Bois would lament that "probably the greatest threat to American education today is the fact that its great and justly celebrated private institutions are supported mainly by their rich graduates: Harvard, Yale, Columbia, Princeton together with smaller institutions like Amherst and Williams are increasingly looked upon as belonging to a certain class in American society: the class of the rich, well-to-do employers, whose interests are more or less opposed to those of the laboring millions. It is because of this unfortunate situation that the clear unhampered study of the industrial process and of economic science has made so little progress in the United States at a time when the critical situation of the modern world calls desperately for such knowledge and teaching." Du Bois, "Future and Function," 185.

15. See Du Bois, "Of Mr. Booker T. Washington," in *Souls of Black Folk*, 33–44.

16. Raymond Williams, *Keywords*, 179.

17. Dewey, "Meaning of Liberalism," 137.

18. Brown, *Undoing the Demos*, 185.

19. Alridge, *Educational Thought of W. E. B. Du Bois*, 103.

20. Watkins, "Marxian and Radical Reconstructionist Critique," 118. As Du Bois put it in 1946: "Education was so arranged that the young learned not necessarily the truth, but that aspect and interpretation of the truth which the rulers of the world wished them to know and follow." *World and Africa*, 16.

21. Du Bois, "Revelation of Saint Orgne," 156.

22. Ibid.

23. Ibid., 158–159.

24. Harding, "Toward the Black University," 157.

25. Du Bois, "Field and Function," 131.

26. Du Bois, *Dusk of Dawn*, 14.

27. Giroux, *Neoliberalism's War on Higher Education*. See Brown, *Undoing the Demos*, 175–200; Donoghue, *Last Professors*; Chatterjee and Maira, *Imperial University*.

28. See Deresiewicz, "Neoliberal Arts"; Jessop, "Cultural Political Economy of Competitiveness"; Hall, *Uberification of the University*. See also Philip Mirowski's reflections on how education has become "a consumer good, not a life-transforming experience," and how this trend has an intellectual basis in the early neoliberal theory of the 1930s. For the neoliberals, he points out, "*Freedom can only be 'negative'* (in the sense of Isaiah Berlin) for one very important reason. Freedom cannot be extended from the use of knowledge *in* society to the use of knowledge *about* society, because self-examination concerning why one passively accepts local and incomplete knowledge leads to contemplation of how market signals create some forms of knowledge and squelch others. Knowledge then assumes global dimensions, and thus undermines the key doctrine of the market as transcendental superior information processor." Philip Mirowski, "Afterword," in Mirowski and Plehwe, *Road from Mont Pèlerin*, 437. Elsewhere, Mirowski points out, quoting Hayek from the 1920s, that "the Market works because it fosters cooperation without dialogue; it works because the values it promotes are noncognitive. The job of education for neoliberals like Hayek is not so much to convey knowledge per se as it is to foster passive acceptance in the hoi polloi toward the infinite wisdom of the Market: 'general education is not solely, and perhaps not even mainly, a matter of the communication of knowledge. There is a need for certain common standards of values.' ... Thus, *ignorance helps promote social order*" (Mirowski, *Never Let a Serious Crisis*, 80, 81).

29. See Newfield, *Unmaking the Public University*, 235, 222.

30. Deresiewicz, "Neoliberal Arts."

31. Brown, *Undoing the Demos*, 181. See also Matthew Stewart's recent commentary on the rise of a "new aristocracy" in American society. "Education—the thing itself, not the degree—is always good," Stewart says. "A genuine education opens minds and makes good citizens. It ought to be pursued *for the sake of society*. In our unbalanced system, however, education has been reduced to a private good, justifiable only by the increments in graduates' paychecks. Instead of uniting and enriching us, it divides and impoverishes." Stewart, "Birth."

32. Giroux, *Neoliberalism's War on Higher Education*, 18, 2. Consider also Lester Spence, who, in his account of the neoliberal turn in Black politics, has argued that nowadays we are "expected to adhere to the values of the market, changing the purpose of education in the process," and "we see African Americans not simply victimized by this transformation but involved in its spread, as the reduction of democratic values that lie at the heart of the neoliberal transformation not only take political power away from black people, it reduces our political imagination to the point where it is difficult for us to even imagine a form of education that isn't solely about increasing one's preparedness for a *job*." Spence, *Knocking the Hustle*, 74.

33. Du Bois, "Field and Function," 156.

34. Deresiewicz, "Neoliberal Arts."

35. Du Bois, "Future and Function," 192. "A dream? Perhaps," Du Bois said in *The World and Africa*, "but even an unrealized dream would be better than the present nightmare" (16).

36. Du Bois, "Field and Function," 122.

37. Du Bois, "Revelation of Saint Orgne," 159; Du Bois, "Where Do We Go from Here?" 156. Eugene Provenzo, quoting a *Crisis* article from 1923 entitled "The Tragedy of Jim Crow," argues that "Du Bois believed that a 'Negro school,' even with its lack of resources and offerings, as an infinitely better place for black children to be than in a place where 'social climbers' could 'make our boys and girls doormats to be spit and trampled upon.'" Provenzo, "Introduction" in Provenzo, *Du Bois on Education*, 15.

38. Du Bois, "Envoy," 162. "No final word is necessary. These are snapshots of my mental states over a period of fifty-two years, a generation of man. They vary from the narrowness of intense conviction to the vagueness of doctrines that attempt universality. They have, however, as I have said before, a certain historic significance. They tell from one point of view, what the American Negro has thought of that education which was designed to fit him as a citizen of modern democracy" (162). Herbert Aptheker, in his introduction to Du Bois's posthumously published *The Education of Black People*, provides a detailed account of the circumstances surrounding Du Bois's efforts to publish an earlier version of the volume with the University of North Carolina Press; for reasons unknown

to Du Bois, that volume, while initially under contract with the Press, never appeared during Du Bois's lifetime (ix–xv).

39. Du Bois, "Revelation of Saint Orgne," 145. It is worth quoting the fuller passage: "In some way, as all intelligent men acknowledge, we must in the end, produce for the satisfaction of human needs and distribute in accordance with human want. To contend that this cannot be done is to face the Impossible Must. The blind cry of reaction on the one hand, which says that we cannot have a planned economy and, therefore, must not try; and the cry of blood, which says that only by force can selfishness be curbed, are equally wrong. It is not a question of deliberate guilt but of selfish stupidity."

40. The question of rationalism in the context of a discussion of Marx is often made to turn on the presumption that racialisms and nationalisms, as purportedly irrational bases of collective identity, will be exposed as such and thus be made to fade away, and of course this sort of rationalist optimism cannot be squared with Du Bois's emphasis on the nature and endurance of racial capitalism. My point is simply that Du Bois works from an implicit narrative about the need to transcend irrationalities in the current moment of human productive and social development. As Nikhil Pal Singh has argued, "Du Bois never conceded his faith in radical Enlightenment universals of human freedom and equality. However, he recognized that these universals had been elaborated *within* and not against the European and American racialization of the world." Singh, *Black Is a Country*, 214.

41. Cedric J. Robinson, *Black Marxism*, 66. Manning Marable has argued similarly that "Du Bois was always aware of the veil of color that inhibited many white radicals from pursuing creative reform strategies challenging racial inequality. He believed that the central contradiction in democratic society was the barrier of racism, and that if left unchallenged, racial prejudice would compromise the goals of social reformers." Marable, *W. E. B. Du Bois*, 84.

42. See Frantz Fanon's famous remark that "Marxian analysis must always be slightly stretched" when it is applied to Black liberation struggles. Fanon, *Wretched of the Earth*, 5.

43. Du Bois, "Future of the Negro State University," 176–177. Du Bois went on to say, "The common cause of the darker races against the intolerable assumptions and insults of Europeans has already found expression. Most men of the world are colored. A belief in humanity means a belief in colored men. The future world will, in all reasonable probability, be what colored men make it. In order for this colored world to come into its heritage must the earth be continuously drenched in the blood of fighting, snarling human beasts? Or will reason and good will prevail? That the latter may be true, the character of the Negro race is the best and greatest hope; for in its normal condition it is at once the strongest

and gentlest of the races of men, but that character can only be raised above emotion to planned reason by institutions such as this may become" (179).

44. In the "Talented Tenth: Memorial Address" [1948], Du Bois noted that "Karl Marx stressed the fact that not merely the upper class but the mass of men were the real people of the world" (349). This reference to the "real people," coupled with a reference to Marx, can likewise be read as a speculative assertion; the idea is that there is still something untrue or irrational about a reality crafted in the image of the "upper class," that a world built by and for the "masses of men" would deliver a truer and more rational, in essence a more real, reality. It is perhaps worth noting, also, that Nahum Dimitri Chandler has sought to read into Du Bois's struggles to set forth "the worlds [he] longed for" a gesture toward impossibility that is not "speculative" in the tradition of European critical theory. "The paradox of becoming other, of becoming oneself as even an encompassment of the other, that takes shape as the way of existence, thought, and practice in this domain, is not produced by way of a speculative disposition toward an idea or an ultimate whole. It is rather in fact a referral to a constitutive order of the possibility of sensibility, being, and existence. This complex passage and the way of inhabitation remains for us, here, now, only by way of this mark, this remainder, perhaps, *of* X." Chandler, *X*, 111. One can see Chandler's point, especially in relation to contemporary debates about ontology—natality, becoming, otherness. If we find ourselves "deposed into a realm of pure speculative anticipation or deduction," we "might hypothesize as pure or situated at the level of a transcendental or of science in the broad sense of thought in general" (61). But this is a searching reading of Du Bois, one that admits of anachronism. Given Du Bois's long-standing Hegelian idealism, given the development narrative that undergirded his mature Marxism, I prefer to refer loosely to a speculative dimension to his mature critical theory. For further reflections on the speculative in Hegel and Du Bois, see Pope, "Ägypten und Aufhebung," and especially Shaw, *W. E. B. Du Bois and "The Souls of Black Folk,"* which provides a comprehensive comparison of Hegel's *Phenomenology of Spirit* and Du Bois's *The Souls of Black Folk*. Surely there is room for further comparison of Hegel's philosophy and the critique that I develop in this book, though given my contextual focus on the 1930s, suffice it to say that Marx's philosophy remains the more fitting point of reference.

45. For a discussion of Du Bois's proposed contribution to Alain Locke's "Bronze Booklets," see Lewis, *W. E. B. Du Bois: The Fight*, 422–426, and Alridge, *Educational Thought of W. E. B. Du Bois*, 88.

46. Du Bois, *Dusk of Dawn*, 159–160. See also Du Bois, *World and Africa*, 162.

47. Editorial, "Collectivism and Collectivism."

48. Provenzo, *Social Frontier*, 10. See also George Counts, "Dare Progressive

Education Be Progressive?" (1932), in which Counts decried education for competition and urged the transition to cooperation.

49. Rugg, "American Scholar Faces," 10. See also Granville Hicks's contribution, which cited as typical an address from a college president who celebrated capitalism and "legitimate competition" as "adherence to the inexorable human laws" (11).

50. Consider Russell Jacoby's commentary, in his review of the French economist Thomas Picketty's best seller, *Capital in the Twenty-First Century*, on compensation trends among top U.S. academic economists. Jacoby notes that Picketty "skewers American academic economists 'many of whom believe that the economy of the United States is working fairly well and, in particular, that it rewards talent and merit accurately and precisely.' This is not surprising, he notes, inasmuch as these economists belong to the top 10 percent of the wealth hierarchy. Their salaries are driven up by the private financial world in which they compete or occasionally work. The result? They 'have the unfortunate tendency to defend their private interests while implausibly claiming to champion the general interest.' Piketty, who taught at MIT, notes in his introduction that the apologist and faux-scientific cast of American economists disillusioned him. A 'great advantage' of being an academic economist in France, Piketty comments, is the minimal respect and pay one receives. This keeps one anchored in the real world." Jacoby, "Picketty v. Marx." Undoubtedly true of academic economists, the same could be said of top researchers across academic disciplines. Although it has not always been the case, nowadays the most visible and influential producers of knowledge in nearly every field regularly draw salaries equal to two, three, even four times the median household income in the United States. As Du Bois might have pointed out, HBCUs buck this trend and thus afford their faculties the same "great advantage" that Picketty found in France.

51. Watkins, "Marxian and Radical Reconstructionist Critique," 124, 127. For further discussion of Du Bois's relationship with the "Reconstructionists," see Alridge, *Educational Thought of W. E. B. Du Bois*, 97–99.

52. Mead, "Problem of Minorities," 243. Within the pages of the *Social Frontier*, there was disagreement about the liberal commitment to the principle of competition. Harry D. Gideonse, who would become the president of Brooklyn College and then chancellor at the New School for Social Research, wrote in 1935 that a "reconstructed liberalism" would "seek such shifts in the institutional setting as will allow a free, that is, competitive situation to emerge again as the ultimately agency of control—that is the genuine liberal position. . . . It would set the public authority against such outgrowths of competition as would end in the destruction of competition. It certainly is not a 'status quo' philosophy." Gideonse, "Non-Partisan Education for Political Intelligence," 59. The point is

that Gideonse is able to fashion himself as a liberal reformer by appealing to a need to challenge a rigged system and set democracy aright, to reconstruct American democracy, by protecting the "freedom" of unfettered competition. We ought to reflect on the advantaged social position from which this argument derives.

53. See Marx, "Letter to Arnold Ruge," 209; Marx and Engels, *Communist Manifesto*, 70.

54. Du Bois, "Talented Tenth."

55. Singh, *Black Is a Country*, 97.

56. It is worth quoting the remainder of Du Bois's passage, which adds further evidentiary support to my argument in this chapter: "He insisted that the masses were poor, ignorant, and sick, not by sin or by nature but by oppression. He preached that planned production of goods and just distribution of income would abolish poverty, ignorance and disease, and make the so-called upper class, not the exception, but the rule among mankind. He declared that the world was not for the few, but for the many; that out of the masses of men could come overwhelming floods of ability and genius, if we freed men by plan and not by rare chance. Civilization not only could be shared by the vast majority of men, but such civilization founded on a wide human base would be better and more enduring than anything that the world has seen. The world would thus escape the enduring danger of being run by a selfish few for their own advantage. Very gradually as the philosophy of Karl Marx and many of his successors seeped into my understanding, I tried to apply this doctrine with regard to Negroes." Du Bois, "The Talented Tenth: Memorial Address," 349.

57. Du Bois, *The Souls of Black Folk*, 37. See also Du Bois, "Where Do We Go from Here?" 156: "Our professional classes are not aristocrats and our masters— they are the most efficient of our servants and thinkers."

58. Shaw, *W. E. B. Du Bois*, 67, 74. For the better-known interpretation that Du Bois ultimately abandoned his Talented Tenth elitism, see Reed, *W. E. B. Du Bois*, and Joy James, *Transcending the Talented Tenth*.

59. See Shaw, *W. E. B. Du Bois*, 73.

60. Du Bois, *In Battle for Peace*, 52. The fuller passage is telling: "In an era like this, and in the United States, many of the educated and gifted young black folk will be as selfish and immoral as the whites who surround them and to whom Negroes have been taught to look as ideals. Naturally, out of the mass of the working classes, who know life and its bitter struggle, will continually rise the real, unselfish and clear-sighted leadership. This will not be automatic or continuous, but the hope of the future of the Negro race in America and the world lies far more among its workers than among its college graduates, *until the time that our higher training is rescued from its sycophantic and cowardly leadership*

of today, almost wholly dependent as it is on Big Business either in politics or philanthropy" (emphasis added).

61. Du Bois, "Talented Tenth."

62. For a discussion of Du Bois's correspondence with Harris and the idea of the "New Spirit College," see Holloway, *Confronting the Veil*, 98.

63. See Du Bois, "Diuturni Silenti"; Lewis, *W. E. B. Du Bois: The Fight*, 132–142; and Alridge, *Educational Thought of W. E. B. Du Bois*, 104.

64. For more on Du Bois's work with the People's College, see Alridge, *Educational Thought of W. E. B. Du Bois*, 98–99, 102–103, and Du Bois and Reid, "Africa and World Freedom."

65. Harding, "Toward the Black University," 158.

66. See Rodney, *Groundings with My Brothers*. For a discussion of Vincent Harding's work with Rodney at the Institute of the Black World in Atlanta the early 1970s, see White, *Challenge of Blackness*.

67. Du Bois, "Future and Function," 191–192. In "The Propaganda of History," the famous parting chapter to *Black Reconstruction*, Du Bois underscored the essentially political nature of knowledge production, a point that he reinforced often in his writings on the Black college. On Du Bois's famous account of how his "career as a scientist was swallowed up in [his] role as a master of propaganda," see Du Bois, *Dusk of Dawn*, 47. One is reminded here of Joel Olson's remark that Du Bois "was a master of propaganda and a scientist, in that order," that he "continued to use the best of scientific research to explain the world, but as a propagandist he . . . used such knowledge (to paraphrase Foucault) for cutting. Du Bois sought to understand the world in order to change it." Olson, "W. E. B. Du Bois and the Race Concept," 214.

68. Harding, "Toward the Black University," 157. For a contemporary defense and appropriation of Harding's thesis, see Myers, "Historically Black College-University."

69. Du Bois, "Field and Function," 126.

70. Ibid., 130–131.

71. Du Bois, *Dusk of Dawn*, 160. Nahum Dimitri Chandler has articulated Du Bois's point in the following way: "There is not now nor has there ever been a free zone or quiet place from which the discourse of so-called Africanist figures, intellectuals, writers, thinkers, or scholars might issue. And this can be shown to be the case in general. Such discourse always emerges in a context and is both a response and a call." Chandler, *X*, 14.

72. It is perhaps worth commenting briefly on what some might regard as an implicit tension between Black Nationalist thinking and that of a disillusioned critic. In a recent commentary on Michael Dawson's categorization of African American political thought, Molefi Kete Asante has decried what he takes to

be the "old traditional canard about Black Nationalism being a response to disillusionment with being outside white America." This, Asante says, "is a total misunderstanding of the legitimate affirmation of culture and respect for identity and heritage that has little or nothing to do with white people." The concern is that an emphasis on disillusionment "is part of an attempt to explain away the dominant ideological current in the black community as only a reaction to not being 'accepted' by whites," and "that readers will never understand the internal agency of those who just plain like being who they are without reacting to anybody else!" Asante, *Afrocentric Manifesto*, 128. Whether or not this is a fair reading of Dawson, surely this is a fair point about the dangers involved in seeing Black culture, identity, and heritage in and through its relation to what Du Bois called the White world. My emphasis on Du Bois's Depression era disillusionment derives from my qualified effort to highlight Du Bois's critique of that White world and its indigenous liberal form. In terms of our appreciation and contemporary appropriation of Du Bois's mature critical theory, we simply must emphasize relations between worlds and the ways in which active and reactive interrelationships shape our sense of the worlds that we inherit and the shared world that we aspire to build, Asante's otherwise excellent points notwithstanding.

73. Du Bois, *Dusk of Dawn*, 160.

74. Angela Y. Davis, *Meaning of Freedom*, 118–119. Harkening back to the discussion in chapter 1 of Eric Porter's analysis of Du Bois's antiracism at midcentury, one is perhaps reminded of Porter's claim that into the 1940s, Du Bois began to develop a complicated line of social criticism, an "antiracism that was simultaneously against racism and color blindness yet committed to investigating fully the logic of each." Porter, *Problem of the Future World*, 23.

75. Obama, "Remarks by the President."

76. Johnson, "President Lyndon B. Johnson's Commencement Address." It is perhaps worth noting that Johnson would go on to lament the "breakdown of the Negro family structure," which was "most important," he said, with "its influence radiating to every part of life."

77. See Obama's 2015 conversation with the writer Marilynne Robinson, whom Obama has credited as one of his favorite authors, but who has recently challenged rather sharply the American celebration of the competitive ethos. Obama and Robinson, "A Conversation—II."

78. As Adolph Reed and Merlin Chowkwanyun have written, the "agenda at work [today] stems from a concern to create competitive individual minority agents who might stand a better fighting chance in the neoliberal rat race rather than a positive alternative vision of a society that eliminates the need to fight constantly against disruptive market whims in the first place. This is a notable

and striking reversal from even the more left-inclined of War on Poverty era liberals, who spoke without shame about moving beyond simply placing people on an equal starting line—'equality of opportunity'—but also making sure they ended up closer to an equal finishing line." Reed and Chowkwanyun, "Race, Class, Crisis," 166.

79. Du Bois (1935) cited in Alridge, *Educational Thought of W. E. B. Du Bois*, 98.

80. Ibid., 99.

81. See Giroux, *Neoliberalism's War on Higher Education*, 2; Dawson, *Blacks In and Out*, 181–182.

82. See Gasman, "W. E. B. Du Bois and Charles S. Johnson."

83. Du Bois, "Field and Function," 128.

Chapter 5. Honoring Dr. Du Bois

1. King, "Honoring Dr. Du Bois," 113, 114, 116–117. The essay was first published by John Henrik Clarke, Esther Jackson, Ernest Kaiser, and J. H. O'Dell, the editors of the journal *Freedomways*, in a volume entitled *Black Titan*. On the point about scholar activism, King goes on to note, "It was never possible to know where the scholar Du Bois ended and the organizer Du Bois began. The two qualities in him were a single unified force" (119).

2. Jackson, *From Civil Rights to Human Rights*, 260. See also Gilens, *Why Americans Hate Welfare*; Gareth Davies, *From Opportunity to Entitlement*; and Hinton, *From the War on Poverty to the War on Crime*, which traces the roots of the carceral state back to the racial narrative surrounding the Great Society programs of the 1960s. For another rich historical account of King's work with the Memphis sanitation workers during the last year of his life, see Honey, *Going Down Jericho Road*.

3. Consider the contemporary writer Marilynne Robinson's observation that if we are committed to the idea that private parties ought to compete with one another, that the prospect of losing incentivizes hard work and personal responsibility, then "poverty is a great asset in this competition, which makes it very improbable indeed that governments will work to raise the living standards or the expectations of their own people" (Robinson, "Fate of Ideas—Competition," 11).

4. King, "SCLC Annual Report," 9. See also Jackson, *From Civil Rights to Human Rights*, 191–195, 260, and Gilens, *Why Americans Hate Welfare*.

5. King, "Seventh Annual Gandhi Memorial Lecture," 10. "The only real revolutionary," King would say a year later, "is a man who has nothing to lose." King, *Trumpet of Conscience*, 60. In regard to deindustrialization and its effects on Black employment prospects, King saw the writing on the wall; consider, for

example, his 1961 speech to the conservative, Cold War era AFL-CIO convention in 1961: "In the next ten to twenty years, automation [and 'relocation of plants'] will grind jobs into the dust as it grinds out unbelievable volumes of production. . . . Hard-core unemployment is now an ugly and unavoidable fact of life." King, "If the Negro Wins," 37.

6. See Denning, "Wageless Life."

7. See Endnotes Editorial Collective, "Brown v. Ferguson." See also Alexander, *New Jim Crow*.

8. See King, "Where Do We Go from Here?" 178.

9. King, "'Cooperative Competition' / 'Noble Competition.'"

10. See, for example, this line, borrowed almost verbatim from Hamilton: "Our first cry as a baby was a bid for attention. And all through childhood the drum major impulse or instinct is a major obsession. Children ask life to grant them first place. They are a little bundle of ego. And they have innately the drum major impulse or the drum major instinct." King, "Drum Major Instinct," 171. It is well known that this was an adaptation of Hamilton's homily, though it is unclear whether or not King had read Hamilton prior to drafting his earlier notes on "'Cooperative Competition' / 'Noble Competition,'" circa 1948–1954. For a discussion of King's indebtedness to Hamilton's sermon, see Keith D. Miller, *Voice of Deliverance*, 3–7.

11. King, "Drum Major Instinct," 171, 185. The conditional quality of King's concluding statement has been the point of contention in the recent controversy surrounding the inscription etched into the King Memorial in Washington, D.C. The poet Maya Angelou and others took issue with an abridged version of the passage, which adorned the memorial when it was first unveiled in 2011. "I was a drum major for justice, peace and righteousness," it said. Angelou responded that this made King look like an "arrogant twit." See Weingarten and Raune, "Maya Angelou." The conditional—"*if you want to say that I was a drum major*"— is key, and this very same grammatical construction appears in King's earlier version, circa 1948–1954: "*If you want to use competition . . .*"

12. Recent efforts to recover a "less sanitized" reading and appropriation of King include West, "Introduction," in *The Radical King*; Jackson, *From Civil Rights to Human Rights*; Glaude, *Democracy in Black*; Angela Y. Davis, *Freedom Is a Constant Struggle*; Taylor, *From #BlackLivesMatter to Black Liberation*, and the essays collected in *Fifty Years since MLK*, edited by Terry and Shelby.

13. King, "Seventh Annual Gandhi Memorial Lecture," 10.

14. Du Bois, "Karl Marx and the Negro Problem Assignments." King frequently iterated this phrase, often with slight variation; it appears, for example, in the Howard University speech: "Seventh Annual Gandhi Memorial Lecture," 9.

15. King, *Where Do We Go from Here?* 182, 187.

16. Ibid., 174; Jackson, *From Civil Rights to Human Rights*, 273.

17. King, *Where Do We Go From Here?* 197. As his former Morehouse College professor Melvin Watson pointed out in a 1953 letter, King misunderstood Marx's materialism. "Marx's position," Watson said, "was that the culture, thoughts, in fact, the whole life of man is conditioned . . . *by the means of production.*" This "variety of materialism is very difficult to refute and is a very disturbing phenomenon," he said, especially for a Baptist preacher steeped in Christian idealism. See Melvin Watson, "Letter to King," 156–157. For a rich set of reflections on King's theorization of political service, including an account of King's critique of a self-serving model, see Rose, *Drum Major Instinct*.

18. King, *Where Do We Go from Here?* 183.

19. King, "Speech at SCLC Staff Retreat"; King, "Doubts and Certainties Link"; and King, *Where Do We Go from Here?* 177–202. See also King's address to the Montgomery Improvement Association in 1955, in which King used almost identical language: "When the history books are written in the future somebody will have to say, 'There lived a race of people, of black people, fleecy locks and black complexion, a people who had the moral courage to stand up for their rights, and thereby they injected a new meaning into the veins of history and of civilization.'" King, "Address to the Initial Mass Meeting," 74. For a discussion of King's use of the "worlds of race" trope, see Baldwin and Dekar, "Becoming 'a Single Neighborhood,'" 27, as well as his discussion in King, *The Trumpet of Conscience*.

20. For a rich discussion of the dehistoricizing tendencies of the contemporary "ethical turn," see Vázquez-Arroyo, *Political Responsibility*.

21. King, "Letter from a Birmingham Jail," 96.

22. Du Bois conveys similar language twice in *Dusk of Dawn*, once in the opening pages, in a passage that I discussed in chapter 2, and then again in the chapter entitled "Revolution," where he says that "beyond my conception of ignorance and deliberate ill-will as causes of race prejudice, there must be other and stronger and more threatening forces, forming the foundations stones of race antagonisms . . . hidden and partially conceived causes of race hate" (141–142).

23. Du Bois, *Dusk of Dawn*, 77.

24. Dawson, *Black Visions*, 275.

25. Adorno, *Minima Moralia*, 39. On the question of despair, it is perhaps worth noting that while Dawson's general point regarding King's later pessimism about American liberal democracy is apt, King continued to guard against giving himself, and allowing others to give themselves, over to a crippling despair. See, for example, King, *Trumpet of Conscience*, 48, where he laments that Black youth in the late 1960s find themselves run up against the prospect of despair as a very real challenge, though he invokes explicitly the legacy of Du Bois in an effort to

motivate a youthful resistance to such an attitude or disposition. Or, as King would remark in his address at the 1968 SCLC staff retreat: "The Negro's disappointment is real, part of the daily menu of our lives. In our individual lives we all too often distill our frustrations into an essence of bitterness or drown ourselves in the deep waters of self-pity or adopt a fatalistic philosophy that whatever happens must happen, that all events are determined by necessity. These reactions poison the soul and scar the personality. The only healthy answer is one's honest recognition of disappointment even as he clings to fragments of hope, the acceptance of finite disappointment while clinging to infinite hope." King, "New Sense of Direction" 10.

26. Engels, "Outline of a Critique of Political Economy," 112.

27. Harrison, "Negro and Socialism," 54. See also Perry, *Hubert Harrison*.

28. King, *Trumpet of Conscience*, 44. On Du Bois's theorization of political rulership, see Gooding-Williams, *In the Shadow of Du Bois*. I have no interest in challenging this reading, though it is worth pointing out that Gooding-Williams deals exclusively with the early Du Bois, with *The Souls of Black Folk* and its turn-of-the-century intellectual context, and does not consider Du Bois's later thinking, including his Depression era critique of liberal theory and his encounter with Marxist thought.

BIBLIOGRAPHY

Adams, James Truslow. *America's Tragedy*. 1934; reprint, New York: Adams, 2007.

——. *The Epic of America*. 1931; reprint, New York: Simon, 2001.

Adorno, Theodor W. *Minima Moralia: Reflections from Damaged Life*. 1951. Translated by E. F. N. Jephcott. New York: Verso, 2005.

Alexander, Michelle. *The New Jim Crow: Mass Incarceration in the Age of Colorblindness*. New York: New Press, 2012.

Allen, Danielle. *Talking to Strangers: Anxieties of Citizenship since Brown v. Board of Education*. Chicago: University of Chicago Press, 2005.

Alridge, Derrick P. *The Educational Thought of W. E. B. Du Bois: An Intellectual History*. New York: Teachers College Press, 2008.

Anderson, Kevin B. *Marx at the Margins: On Nationalism, Ethnicity, and Non-Western Societies*. Chicago: University of Chicago Press, 2010.

Anderson, Patrick. "Pan-Africanism and Economic Nationalism: W. E. B. Du Bois's *Black Reconstruction* and the Failings of the 'Black Marxism' Thesis." *Journal of Black Studies* 43, no. 8 (November 2017): 732–757.

Appiah, Kwame Anthony. *In My Father's House: Africa in the Philosophy of Culture*. New York: Oxford University Press, 1992.

——. *Lines of Descent: W. E. B. Du Bois and the Emergence of Identity*. Cambridge: Harvard University Press, 2014.

——. "The Uncompleted Argument: Du Bois and the Illusion of Race." *Critical Inquiry* 12, no. 1 (Autumn 1985): 21–37.

Aptheker, Herbert, ed. *The Education of Black People: Ten Critiques, 1906–1960*. New York: Monthly Review, 2001.

Asante, Molefi Kete. *An Afrocentric Manifesto: Toward an African Renaissance*. Malden, Mass.: Polity Press, 2008.

Baldwin, Kate A. *Beyond the Color Line and the Iron Curtain: Reading Encounters between Black and Red, 1922–1963*. Durham, N.C.: Duke University Press, 2002.

Baldwin, Lewis V., and Paul R. Dekar. "Becoming 'a Single Neighborhood': Martin Luther King Jr. on the 'White' and 'Colored' Worlds." In *"In an Inescapable Network of Mutuality": Martin Luther King Jr. and the*

Globalization of an Ethical Ideal, edited by Lewis V. Baldwin and Paul R. Dekar. Eugene, Ore.: Cascade Books, 2013.

Balfour, Lawrie. *Democracy's Reconstruction: Thinking Politically with W. E. B. Du Bois*. New York: Oxford University Press, 2011.

Bell, Duncan. "What Is Liberalism?" *Political Theory* 42, no. 6 (2014): 682–715.

Bogues, Anthony. *Empire of Liberty: Power, Desire, and Freedom*. Lebanon, N.H.: Dartmouth College Press, 2010.

Boltanski, Luc, and Eve Chiapello. *The New Spirit of Capitalism*. Translated by Gregory Elliott. New York: Verso, 2007.

Boustan, Leah Platt. *Competition in the Promised Land: Black Migrants in Northern Cities and Labor Markets*. Princeton, N.J.: Princeton University Press, 2016.

Brenner, Robert. *Merchants and Revolution: Commercial Change, Political Conflict, and London's Overseas Traders, 1550–1653*. New York, Verso, 2003.

Brown, Wendy. *Undoing the Demos: Neoliberalism's Stealth Revolution*. Cambridge, Mass.: Zone Books, 2015.

Burgin, Angus. *The Great Persuasion: Reinventing Free Markets since the Depression*. Cambridge: Harvard University Press, 2012.

Chandler, Nahum Dimitri. *X—The Problem of the Negro as a Problem for Thought*. New York: Fordham University Press, 2015.

Chatterjee, Piya, and Sunaina Maira, eds. *The Imperial University: Academic Repression and Scholarly Dissent*. Minneapolis: University of Minnesota Press, 2014.

Clarke, John Henrik, Esther Jackson, Ernest Kaiser, and J. H. O'Dell. *Black Titan: W. E. B. Du Bois*. Boston: Beacon Press, 1970.

Clarno, Andy. *Neoliberal Apartheid: Palestine/Israel and South Africa after 1994*. Chicago: University of Chicago Press, 2017.

Cleaver, Harry. *Reading* Capital *Politically*. San Francisco: AK Press, 2000.

Coates, Ta-Nehisi. *Between the World and Me*. New York: Spiegel and Grau, 2015.

Counts, George. "Dare Progressive Education Be Progressive?" *Progressive Education* 9, no. 4 (February 1932): 257–263.

Dardot, Pierre, and Christian Laval. *The New Way of the World: On Neoliberal Society*. Translated by Gregory Elliott. New York: Verso, 2017.

Davidson, Neil. "Is There Anything to Defend in Political Marxism?" *International Socialist Review* 91 (January/February 2014).

Davies, Gareth. *From Opportunity to Entitlement: The Transformation and Decline of Great Society Liberalism*. Lawrence: University Press of Kansas, 1996.

Davies, William. *The Limits of Neoliberalism: Authority, Sovereignty, and the Logic of Competition*. Thousand Oaks, Calif.: Sage, 2014.

Davis, Angela Y. *Freedom Is a Constant Struggle: Ferguson, Palestine, and the Foundations of a Movement*. San Francisco: City Lights Press, 2016.

———. *The Meaning of Freedom and Other Difficult Dialogues*. San Francisco: City Lights Press, 2012.

Davis, David Brion. *The Problem of Slavery in the Age of Revolution: 1770–1823*. New York: Oxford University Press, 1999.

Dawson, Michael C. *Black Visions: The Roots of Contemporary African American Political Ideologies*. Chicago: University of Chicago Press, 2001.

———. *Blacks In and Out of the Left*. Cambridge: Harvard University Press, 2013.

———. "Hidden in Plain Sight: A Note on Legitimation Crises and the Racial Order." *Critical Historical Studies* (Spring 2016): 143–161.

Dawson, Michael C., and Megan Ming Francis. "Black Politics and the Neoliberal Racial Order." *Public Culture* 28, no. 1 (2016): 23–62.

Denning, Michael. "Wageless Life." *New Left Review* 66 (November/December 2010): 70–97.

Deresiewicz, William. "The Neoliberal Arts: How College Sold Its Soul to the Market." *Harper's Magazine*, September 2015, 25–32.

Dewey, John. "The Meaning of Liberalism." 1935. In *The Social Frontier: A Critical Reader*, edited by Eugene Provenzo Jr. New York: Peter Lang, 2011.

Donoghue, Frank. *The Last Professors: The Corporate University and the Fate of the Humanities*. New York: Fordham University Press, 2008.

Douglas, Andrew J. "Diagnosing Racial Capitalism." In *Fifty Years since MLK*, edited by Brandon M. Terry, 40–44. Cambridge: Boston Review / MIT Press, 2018.

Douglass, Frederick. *The Narrative of the Life of Frederick Douglass, an American Slave: Written by Himself*. 1845. Reprint edited by John R. McKivigan IV, Peter P. Hinks, and Heather L. Kaufman. New Haven, Conn.: Yale University Press, 2016.

Du Bois, W. E. B. *Black Reconstruction in America: 1860–1880*. 1935; reprint, New York: Free Press, 1998.

———. "The Class Struggle." 1921. In Lewis, *W. E. B. Du Bois: A Reader*, 555–556.

———. "The Conservation of the Races." 1897. In Huggins, *Writings*, 815–826.

———. "Consumers' Co-operation." *Crisis* 17 (January 1919).

———. *The Correspondence of W. E. B. Du Bois*. Vol. 2. Edited by Herbert Aptheker. Amherst: University of Massachusetts Press, 1997.

———. *Darkwater: Voices from within the Veil*. 1920; reprint, New York: Oxford University Press, 2007.

———. "Diuturni Silenti." 1924. In Aptheker, *Education of Black People*, 61–84.

———. *Dusk of Dawn: An Essay toward an Autobiography of a Race Concept*. 1940; reprint, New York: Oxford University Press, 2014.

———. "Education and Work." 1930. In Aptheker, *Education of Black People*, 85–110.

———. "Envoy." 1940. In Aptheker, *Education of Black People*, 162.

———. "The Evolution of the Race Problem." 1909. In *W. E. B. Du Bois Speaks: Speeches and Writings, 1890–1919*, edited by Philip S. Foner, 209–224. New York: Pathfinder Press, 1970.

———. "The Field and Function of the Negro College." 1933. In Aptheker, *Education of Black People*, 111–134.

———. "The Future and Function of the Private Negro College." 1946. In Aptheker, *Education of Black People*, 181–192.

———. "The Future of the Negro State University." 1941. In Aptheker, *Education of Black People*, 169–180.

———. *In Battle for Peace: The Story of My 83rd Birthday*. 1952; reprint, New York: Oxford University Press, 2014.

———. "Marxism and the Negro Problem." 1933. In Lewis, *W. E. B. Du Bois: A Reader*, 538–544.

———. "Karl Marx and the Negro Problem Assignments." 1933. Du Bois Papers, MS 312, Special Collections and University Archives, University of Massachusetts, Amherst.

———. "Letter to Matthew V. Boutte, March 13, 1933." In David Levering Lewis, *W. E. B. Du Bois: The Fight for Equality and the American Century, 1919–1963*. New York: Henry Holt, 2000.

———. "My Evolving Program for Negro Freedom." 1944. In *What the Negro Wants*, edited by Rayford W. Logan, 31–70. South Bend, Ind.: University of Notre Dame Press, 2001.

———. "The Negro and Social Reconstruction." 1936. In *Against Racism: Unpublished Essays, Papers, Addresses, 1887–1961*, edited by Herbert Aptheker. Amherst: University of Massachusetts Press, 1988.

———. "A Negro Nation within the Nation." 1935. In Lewis, *W. E. B. Du Bois: A Reader*, 563–570.

———. *The Philadelphia Negro: A Social Study*. 1899. Reprint, New York: Oxford University Press, 2014.

———. "The Revelation of Saint Orgne the Damned." 1938. In Aptheker, *Education of Black People*, 135–162.

———. "Segregation in the North." 1934. In Huggins, *Writings*, 1239–1247.

———. *The Souls of Black Folk*. 1903; reprint, New York: Oxford University Press, 2014.

———. "The Study of the Negro Problems." *Annals of the American Academy of Political and Social Science* 11, no. 1 (1898): 1–23.

——. *The Suppression of the African Slave-Trade*. 1896; reprint, New York: Oxford University Press, 2014.

——. "The Talented Tenth: Memorial Address." 1948. In Lewis, *W. E. B. Du Bois: A Reader*, 347–353.

——. "A Vacation Unique." 1889. In Shamoon Zamir, *Dark Voices: W. E. B. Du Bois and American Thought, 1888–1903*. Chicago: University of Chicago Press, 1995.

——. W. E. B. Du Bois to Harris, January 27, 1931. Du Bois Papers.

——. W. E. B. Du Bois to Harris, January 6, 1933. Du Bois Papers.

——. *W. E. B. Du Bois: A Reader*. Edited by David Levering Lewis. New York: Henry Holt, 1995.

——. "'Where Do We Go from Here?' (A Lecture on Negroes' Economic Plight): An Address Delivered at the Rosenwald Economic Conference in Washington, D.C., May 1933." In *A W. E. B. Du Bois Reader*, edited by Andrew Paschal. 146–163. New York: Macmillan, 1971.

——. *The World and Africa*. 1946; reprint, New York: Oxford University Press, 2007.

——. *Writings*. Edited by Nathan Huggins. New York: Viking Press, 1986.

Du Bois, W. E. B., and Ira De A. Reid. "Africa and World Freedom." *Phylon* 4 (1943): 8–12.

Editorial. "Collectivism and Collectivism." *Social Frontier* 1, no. 1 (1934): 3–4.

Eley, Geoff. "Historicizing the Global, Politicizing Capital: Giving the Present a Name." *History Workshop Journal* 63 (2007): 154–188.

Endnotes Collective. *Endnotes 2: Misery and the Value-Form*. Oakland, Calif.: AK Press, 2010.

Endnotes Editorial Collective. "Brown v. Ferguson." *Endnotes 4: Unity in Separation*. 2015. https://endnotes.org.uk/issues/4/en/endnotes-brown-v-ferguson, accessed September 30, 2016.

Engels, Friedrich. "Outline of a Critique of Political Economy." 1844. Quoted in Terrell Carver, *Engels: His Life and Thought*. New York: Palgrave Macmillan, 1990.

Fanon, Frantz. *The Wretched of the Earth*. 1961; reprint, New York: Grove Press, 2007.

Foucault, Michel. *The Birth of Biopolitics: Lectures at the Collège de France, 1978–1979*. Translated by Graham Burchell. New York: Picador, 2008.

Fraser, Nancy. "Behind Marx's Hidden Abode: For an Expanded Conception of Capitalism." *New Left Review* 86 (2014): 55–72.

——. "Expropriation and Exploitation in Racialized Capitalism: A Reply to Michael Dawson." *Critical Historical Studies* 3, no. 1 (Spring 2016): 163–178.

Gasman, Marybeth. "W. E. B. Du Bois and Charles S. Johnson: Differing

Views on the Role of Philanthropy in Higher Education." *Higher Education Quarterly* 42, no. 4 (December 2002): 493–516.

Geuss, Raymond. *The Idea of a Critical Theory: Habermas and the Frankfurt School.* New York: Cambridge University Press, 1981.

———. *Philosophy and Real Politics.* Princeton, N.J.: Princeton University Press, 2008.

Gideonse, Harry D. "Non-Partisan Education for Political Intelligence." 1935. In *The Social Frontier: A Critical Reader,* edited by Eugene Provenzo Jr. New York: Peter Lang, 2010.

Gilbert, Jeremy. "What Kind of Thing Is 'Neoliberalism'?" *New Formations* 80/81 (2013): 7–22.

Gilens, Martin. *Why Americans Hate Welfare: Race, Media, and the Politics of Antipoverty Policy.* Chicago: University of Chicago Press, 1999.

Gilmore, Glenda E. *Defying Dixie: The Radical Roots of Civil Rights.* New York: Norton, 2008.

Giroux, Henry A. *Neoliberalism's War on Higher Education.* Chicago: Haymarket, 2014.

Gilroy, Paul. *The Black Atlantic: Modernity and Double Consciousness.* New York: Verso, 1993.

Glaude, Eddie S. *Democracy in Black: How Race Still Enslaves the American Soul.* New York: Crown, 2016.

Goldberg, David Theo. *Sites of Race: Conversations with Susan Searls Giroux.* Malden, Mass.: Polity Press, 2014.

Gooding-Williams, Robert. *In the Shadow of Du Bois: Afro-Modern Political Thought in America.* Cambridge: Harvard University Press, 2009.

Gorman, William. "W. E. B. Du Bois and His Work." *Fourth International* 11, no. 3 (May/June 1950): 80–86.

Gunnell, John. "The Archeology of American Liberalism." *Journal of Political Ideologies* 6 (2001): 125–145.

———. *Imagining the American Polity.* Philadelphia: Pennsylvania State University Press, 2004.

Hall, Gary. *The Uberification of the University.* Minneapolis: University of Minnesota Press, 2016.

Harding, Vincent. "Toward the Black University." *Ebony* 25 (August 1970): 156–159.

Harney, Stefano, and Fred Moten. *The Undercommons: Fugitive Planning and Black Study.* New York: Minor Compositions, 2013.

Harris, Abram, Jr. "Future Plan and Program of the NAACP." 1934. NAACP Papers, Library of Congress.

———. Harris to Du Bois, January 7, 1933. W. E. B. Du Bois Papers (MS 312).

Special Collections and University Archives, University of Massachusetts
Amherst Libraries.

———. Letter to Calverton, April 6, 1925. V. F. Calverton Papers, Manuscripts
and Archives Division, New York Public Library.

———. "Reconstruction and the Negro." 1935. In *Race, Radicalism, and
Reform: Selected Papers of Abram Harris*, edited by William Darity Jr. New
Brunswick, N.J.: Transaction, 1989: 209–212.

Harris, Abram, Jr., and Sterling Spero. *The Black Worker: The Negro and the
Labor Movement*. 1931; reprint, Port Washington, N.Y.: Kennikat Press, 1966.

Harrison, Hubert. "The Negro and Socialism: I—The Negro Problem Stated."
1911. In *A Hubert Harrison Reader*, edited by Jeffrey B. Perry. Middletown,
Conn.: Wesleyan University Press, 2001.

Harvey, David. *A Brief History of Neoliberalism*. New York: Oxford University
Press, 2007.

———. *A Companion to Marx's "Capital."* Vol. 1. New York: Oxford University
Press, 2010.

———. *The Enigma of Capital and the Crises of Capitalism*. New York: Oxford
University Press, 2011.

———. *Marx, Capital, and the Madness of Economic Reason*. New York: Oxford
University Press, 2017.

———. *Seventeen Contradictions and the End of Capitalism*. New York: Oxford
University Press, 2015.

Hicks, Granville. "The Captive School." *Social Frontier* 2, no. 1 (1935): 10–12.

Hinton, Elizabeth. *From the War on Poverty to the War on Crime: The Making of
Mass Incarceration in America*. Cambridge: Harvard University Press, 2016.

Holloway, Jonathan Scott. *Confronting the Veil: Abram Harris Jr., E. Franklin
Frazier, and Ralph Bunche, 1919–1941*. Chapel Hill: University of North
Carolina Press, 2002.

Honey, Michael K. *Going Down Jericho Road: The Memphis Strike: Martin Luther
King's Last Campaign*. New York: Norton, 2007.

Hook, Sidney. *Towards the Understanding of Karl Marx: A Revolutionary
Interpretation*. 1933; reprint, New York: Prometheus Books, 2002.

Horne, Gerald. *Black and Red: W. E. B. Du Bois and the Afro-American Response
to the Cold War*. Albany: State University of New York Press, 1986.

Huggins, Nathan, ed. *Writings*, by W. E. B. Du Bois. New York: Viking Press, 1986.

Jackson, Thomas F. *From Civil Rights to Human Rights: Martin Luther King
Jr. and the Struggle for Economic Justice*. Philadelphia: University of
Pennsylvania Press, 2007.

Jacoby, Russell. *The Black Jacobins: Toussaint L'Ouverture and the San Domingo
Revolution*. 1938; reprint, New York: Vintage, 1989.

——. "Dialectical Materialism and the Fate of Humanity." 1947. In *The C. L. R. James Reader*, edited by Anna Grimshaw. Cambridge, Mass.: Blackwell, 1992.

——. "Picketty v. Marx." *New Republic*, June 7, 2014.

James, C. L. R. "African Independence and the Myth of African Inferiority." In *Education and Black Struggle: Notes from the Colonized World*, edited by the Institute of the Black World. Cambridge: Harvard Educational Review, 1974.

James, Joy. *Transcending the Talented Tenth: Black Leaders and American Intellectuals*. New York: Routledge, 1997.

Jessop, Bob. "The Cultural Political Economy of Competitiveness and Its Implications for Higher Education." In *The Knowledge Economy and Lifelong Learning: A Critical Reader*, edited by D. W. Livingstone and David Guile, 57–83. Rotterdam: Sense, 2012.

Johnson, Lyndon B. "President Lyndon B. Johnson's Commencement Address at Howard University: 'To Fulfill These Rights,' June 4, 1965." http://www .lbjlib.utexas.edu/johnson/archives.hom/speeches.hom/650604.asp, accessed June 3, 2016.

Johnson, Theresa Gaye, and Alex Lubin, eds. *Futures of Black Radicalism*. New York: Verso, 2017.

Johnson, Walter. "To Remake the World: Slavery, Racial Capitalism, and Justice." In Johnson and Kelley, *Race, Capitalism, Justice*, 11–31.

Johnson, Walter, and Robin D. G. Kelley, eds. *Race, Capitalism, Justice*. Cambridge: Boston Review / MIT Press, 2017.

Jones, Daniel Stedman. *Masters of the Universe: Hayek, Freidman, and the Birth of Neoliberal Politics*. Princeton, N.J.: Princeton University Press, 2012.

Katznelson, Ira. *Fear Itself: The New Deal and the Origins of Our Time*. New York: Norton, 2013.

——. *When Affirmative Action Was White: An Untold History of Racial Inequality in America*. New York: Norton, 2006.

Kelley, Robin D. G. *Freedom Dreams: The Black Radical Imagination*. Boston: Beacon, 2002.

King, Martin Luther, Jr. "Address to the Initial Mass Meeting of the Montgomery Improvement Association." 1955. In *The Papers of Martin Luther King Jr., Vol. II: Rediscovering Precious Values, July 1951–November 1955*, edited by Clayborne Carson, Ralph E. Luker, Penny A. Russell, and Pete Holloran. Berkeley: University of California Press, 1994.

——. "'Cooperative Competition' / 'Noble Competition.'" 1948–1954. In *The Papers of Martin Luther King Jr., Vol. IV: Advocate of the Social Gospel, September 1948–March 1963*, edited by Clayborne Carson, 583–584. Berkeley: University of California Press, 2007.

——. "Doubts and Certainties Link: A Transcript of an Interview with Martin Luther King Jr." 1968. Library and Archives for the Martin Luther King Jr. Center for Nonviolent Social Change, Atlanta.

——. "The Drum Major Instinct." 1968. In *A Knock at Midnight: Inspiration from the Great Sermons of Reverend Martin Luther King Jr.*, edited by Clayborne Carson and Peter Holloran. New York: Warner Books, 2000.

——. "Honoring Dr. Du Bois." 1968; reprint in *The Radical King*, edited by Cornel West. Boston: Beacon Press, 2015.

——. "If the Negro Wins, Labor Wins." 1961. In *"All Labor Has Dignity,"* edited by Michael K. Honey, 37–45. Boston: Beacon, 2011.

——. "Letter from a Birmingham Jail." 1963. In *Why We Can't Wait*. Boston: Beacon, 2011.

——. "A New Sense of Direction." 1968. *Worldview*, April 1972, 5–12.

——. "SCLC Annual Report." 1965. Library and Archives for the Martin Luther King Jr. Center for Nonviolent Social Change, Atlanta.

——. "Seventh Annual Gandhi Memorial Lecture, Howard University." November 6, 1966. Library and Archives for the Martin Luther King Jr. Center for Nonviolent Social Change, Atlanta.

——. "Speech at SCLC Staff Retreat." 1966. Library and Archives for the Martin Luther King Jr. Center for Nonviolent Social Change, Atlanta.

——. *The Trumpet of Conscience*. 1967; reprint, Boston: Beacon Press, 2010.

——. *Where Do We Go from Here: Chaos or Community?* 1967; reprint, Boston: Beacon Press, 2010.

Latour, Bruno. "Why Has Critique Run Out of Steam? From Matters of Fact to Matters of Concern." *Critical Inquiry* 30 (Winter 2004): 225–248.

Lewis, David Levering. *W. E. B. Du Bois: Biography of a Race, 1868–1919*. New York: Henry Holt, 1993.

——. *W. E. B. Du Bois: The Fight for Equality and the American Century, 1919–1963*. New York: Henry Holt, 2000.

——, ed. *W. E. B. Du Bois: A Reader*. New York: Henry Holt, 1995.

Locke, John. *Two Treatises of Government*. 1691; reprint, New York: Cambridge University Press, 1994.

Losurdo, Domenico. *Liberalism: A Counter-History*. New York: Verso, 2014.

Madison, James. "The Federalist No. 51." 1788. In Alexander Hamilton, James Madison, and John Jay, *The Federalist Papers*, edited by Ian Shapiro. New Haven: Yale University Press, 2009.

Marable, Manning. *W. E. B. Du Bois: Black Radical Democrat*. 1986; reprint, New York: Routledge, 2005.

Marasco, Robyn. *The Highway of Despair: Critical Theory after Hegel*. New York: Columbia University Press, 2015.

Marx, Karl. *Capital.* Vol. 1, *A Critique of Political Economy.* 1867; reprint, New
    York: Penguin, 1992.
———. "The Eighteenth Brumaire of Louis Bonaparte." 1852. In *The Marx-Engels
    Reader,* edited by Robert Tucker, 594–617. New York: Norton, 1977.
———. *Grunrdrisse: Foundations of the Critique of Political Economy.* 1857–1858;
    reprint, New York: Penguin, 1993.
———. "Letter to Arnold Ruge, September 1843." In *Karl Marx: Early Writings*,
    translated by Rodney Livingstone and Gregor Benton. New York: Penguin,
    1992.
———. Marx to Engels, June 18, 1862. https://marxists.catbull.com/archive/
    marx/works/1862/letters/62_06_18.htm, accessed June 25, 2018.
———. *The Poverty of Philosophy.* 1847; reprint, New York: Prometheus Books,
    1995.
Marx, Karl, and Friedrich Engels. *The Communist Manifesto.* 1848; reprint, New
    York: Penguin, 2002.
———. *The German Ideology.* 1845; reprint, New York: Prometheus Books, 1998.
McCarthy, Jesse. "The Low End Theory: Fred Moten's Subversive Black Studies
    Scholarship." *Harvard Magazine,* January–February 2018.
Mead, Margaret. "The Problem of Minorities." Undated. In *The Social Frontier: A
    Critical Reader,* edited by Eugene Provenzo Jr. New York: Peter Lang, 2010.
Mehta, Uday Singh. *Liberalism and Empire: A Study in Nineteenth-Century
    British Liberal Thought.* Chicago: University of Chicago Press, 1999.
Melamed, Jodi. "Racial Capitalism." *Critical Ethnic Studies* 1, no. 1 (Spring 2015):
    76–85.
Miller, Eben. *Born along the Color Line: The 1933 Amenia Conference and the Rise
    of a National Civil Rights Movement.* New York: Oxford University Press, 2012.
Miller, Keith D. *Voice of Deliverance: The Language of Martin Luther King Jr. and
    Its Sources.* Athens: University of Georgia Press, 1998.
Mills, Charles W. "Racial Liberalism." *PMLA* 132, no. 5 (2008): 1380–1397.
Mirowski, Philip. *Never Let a Serious Crisis Go to Waste: How Neoliberalism
    Survived the Financial Meltdown.* New York: Verso, 2014.
Mirowski, Philip, and Dieter Plehwe, eds. *The Road from Mont Pèlerin: The
    Making of the Neoliberal Thought Collective.* Cambridge: Harvard University
    Press, 2015.
Morgan, Lynda J. *Known for My Work: African American Ethics from Slavery to
    Freedom.* Gainesville: University Press of Florida, 2016.
Moses, Wilson Jeremiah. *Afrotopia: The Roots of African American Popular
    History.* New York: Cambridge University Press, 1998.
Mullen, Bill V. *Un-American: W. E. B. Du Bois and the Century of World
    Revolution.* Philadelphia: Temple University Press, 2015.

Myers, Joshua. "The Historically Black College-University: Of Vision and Memory / 'Dark Copies of Dying Whiteness Are No Longer Needed.'" *Liberator Magazine*, July 2014.

Nembhard, Jessica Gordon. "Cooperative Ownership in the Struggle for African American Economic Empowerment." *Humanity and Society* 28, no. 3 (2004): 298–321.

Newfield, Christopher. *Unmaking the Public University: The Forty-Year Assault on the Middle Class*. Cambridge: Harvard University Press, 2008.

Obama, Barack. "Remarks by the President at Morehouse College Commencement Ceremony." 2013. https://www.whitehouse.gov/the-press-office/2013/05/19/remarks-president-morehouse-college-commencement-ceremony, accessed June 3, 2016.

Obama, Barack, and Marilynne Robinson. "President Obama and Marilynne Robinson: A Conversation—II." *New York Review of Books*, November 19, 2015.

Olson, Joel. *The Abolition of White Democracy*. Minneapolis: University of Minnesota Press, 2004.

———. "W. E. B. Du Bois and the Race Concept." In *Racially Writing the Republic: Racists, Race Rebels, and Transformations of American Identity*, edited by Bruce Baum, Duchess Harris, and John Kuo Wei Tchen, 214–230. Durham, N.C.: Duke University Press, 2009.

Peck, Jamie. *Constructions of Neoliberal Reason*. New York: Oxford University Press, 2013.

Perelman, Michael. *The Invention of Capitalism: Classical Political Economy and the Secret History of Primitive Accumulation*. Durham, N.C.: Duke University Press, 2000.

Perry, Jeffrey Babcock. *Hubert Harrison: The Voice of Harlem Radicalism, 1883–1918*. New York: Columbia University Press, 2009.

Picketty, Thomas. *Capital in the Twenty-First Century*. Cambridge: Harvard University Press, 2014.

Pope, Jeremy. "Ägypten und Aufhebung: G. W. F. Hegel, W. E. B. Du Bois, and the African Orient." *CR: The New Centennial Review* 6, no. 3 (Winter 2006): 149–192.

Porter, Eric. *The Problem of the Future World: W. E. B. Du Bois and the Race Concept at Midcentury*. Durham, N.C.: Duke University Press, 2010.

Post, Charles. *The American Road to Capitalism: Studies in Class-Structure, Economic Development, and Political Conflict, 1620–1877*. Chicago: Haymarket Books, 2012.

Provenzo, Eugene, Jr., ed. *Du Bois on Education*. New York: AltaMira Press, 2002.

———, ed. *The Social Frontier: A Critical Reader*. New York: Peter Lang, 2010.

Reed, Adolph, Jr. "The 'Color Line' Then and Now: *The Souls of Black Folk*
and the Changing Context of Black American Politics." In *Renewing Black
Intellectual History: The Ideological and Material Foundations of African
American Thought*, edited by Adolph Reed Jr. and Kenneth W. Warren.
Boulder: Paradigm, 2010.

———. *W. E. B. Du Bois and American Political Thought: Fabianism and the Color
Line*. New York: Oxford University Press, 1997.

Reed, Adolph, and Merlin Chowkwanyun. "Race, Class, Crisis: The Discourse of
Racial Disparity and Its Analytical Discontents." *Socialist Register* 48 (2012):
149–175.

Roberts, Neil. *Freedom as Marronage*. Chicago: University of Chicago Press,
2015.

Robinson, Cedric J. *Black Marxism: The Making of the Black Radical Tradition*.
1983; reprint, Chapel Hill: University of North Carolina Press, 2000.

———. "Oliver Cromwell Cox and the Historiography of the West." *Cultural
Critique*, no. 17 (Winter 1990–1991): 5–19.

Robinson, Marilynne. "The Fate of Ideas—Competition." *Salmagundi*, no.
148/149 (Fall 2005–Winter 2006): 3–15.

Rodney, Walter. *Groundings with My Brothers*. London: Bogle-L'Ouverture, 1969.

Roediger, David. *Seizing Freedom: Slave Emancipation and Liberty for All*. New
York: Verso, 2014.

Rose, Justin. *The Drum Major Instinct: Martin Luther King Jr.'s Theory of Political
Service*. Athens: University of Georgia Press, 2019.

Rosen, Michael. *On Voluntary Servitude: False Consciousness and the Theory of
Ideology*. Cambridge: Harvard University Press, 1996.

———. "*On Voluntary Servitude* and the Theory of Ideology." *Constellations* 7, no.
3 (2000): 393–407.

Rugg, Harold. "The American Scholar Faces a Social Crisis." *Social Frontier* 1,
no. 6 (1935): 10–13.

Sabine, George. *A History of Political Theory*. New York: Henry Holt, 1951.

Sala-Molins, Louis. *Dark Side of the Light: Slavery and the French Enlightenment*.
Minneapolis: University of Minnesota Press, 2006.

Schumpeter, Joseph A. *Capitalism, Socialism, and Democracy*. 1942; reprint,
New York: Harper Perennial, 2008.

———. *The Theory of Economic Development: An Inquiry into Profits, Capital,
Credit, Interest, and the Business Cycle*. 1911; reprint, Cambridge: Harvard
University Press, 1934.

Shaw, Stephanie J. *W. E. B. Du Bois and "The Souls of Black Folk."* Chapel Hill:
University of North Carolina Press, 2013.

Singh, Nikhil Pal. *Black Is a Country: Race and the Unfinished Struggle for Democracy.* Cambridge: Harvard University Press, 2005.

———. "On Race, Violence, and So-Called Primitive Accumulation." *Social Text 128,* 34, no. 3 (September 2016): 27–50.

———. *Race and America's Long War.* Oakland: University of California Press, 2017.

Smallwood, Stephanie. "What Slavery Tells Us about Marx." In Johnson and Kelley, *Race, Capitalism, Justice,* 78–82.

Smith, Adam. *The Wealth of Nations: Books I–III.* 1776; reprint, New York: Penguin, 1999.

Spence, Lester K. *Knocking the Hustle: Against the Neoliberal Turn in Black Politics.* New York: Punctum Books, 2015.

Stewart, Matthew. "The Birth of a New American Aristocracy." *Atlantic,* June 2018.

Streator, George. "April 8, 1935 Letter to Du Bois." In *The Correspondence of W. E. B. Du Bois,* vol. 2, edited by Herbert Aptheker. Amherst: University of Massachusetts Press, 1997.

Streek, Wolfgang. *How Will Capitalism End? Essays on a Failing System.* New York: Verso, 2017.

Taylor, Keeanga-Yamahtta. *From #BlackLivesMatter to Black Liberation.* Chicago: Haymarket, 2016.

———. "W. E. B. Du Bois: Black Reconstruction in America, 1860–1880." *International Socialist Review* 57 (January/February 2008).

Terry, Brandon M., and Tommie Shelby. *Fifty Years since MLK.* Cambridge: Boston Review / MIT Press, 2018.

Thiel, Peter. "Competition Is for Losers." *Wall Street Journal,* September 14, 2014.

Van Wienen, Mark W. *American Socialist Triptych: The Literary-Political Work of Charlotte Perkins Gilman, Upton Sinclair, and W. E. B. Du Bois.* Ann Arbor: University of Michigan Press, 2012.

Vázquez-Arroyo, Antonio Y. *Political Responsibility: Responding to Predicaments of Power.* New York: Columbia University Press, 2016.

Watkins, William H. "A Marxian and Radical Reconstructionist Critique of American Education: Searching Out Black Voices." In *Black Protest Thought and Education,* edited by William H. Watkins. New York: Peter Lang, 2011.

Watson, Melvin. "Letter to King," August 14, 1952. In *The Papers of Martin Luther King Jr., Vol. II: Rediscovering Precious Values, July 1951–November 1955,* edited by Clayborne Carson and Peter H. Holloran, 156–157. Berkeley: University of California Press, 1994.

Weingarten, Gene, and Michael R. Raune. "Maya Angelou Says King Memorial Inscription Makes Him Look 'Arrogant.'" *Washington Post,* August 30, 2011.

West, Cornel, ed. *The Radical King*. Boston: Beacon, 2015.

White, Derrick E. *The Challenge of Blackness: The Institute of the Black World and Political Activism in the 1970s*. Gainesville: University Press of Florida, 2011.

Williams, Eric. *Capitalism and Slavery*. 1944; reprint, Chapel Hill: University of North Carolina Press, 1994.

Williams, Raymond. *Keywords: A Vocabulary of Culture and Society*. New York: Oxford University Press, 2015.

Winant, Howard. *The World Is a Ghetto: Race and Democracy since World War II*. New York: Basic Books, 2001.

Wood, Ellen Meiksins. *The Origin of Capitalism: A Longer View*. New York: Verso, 2002.

Zamir, Shamoon. *Dark Voices: W. E. B. Du Bois and American Thought, 1888–1903*. Chicago: University of Chicago Press, 1995.

Zimmerman, Andrew. "When Liberals Defended Slavery." In Johnson and Kelley, *Race, Capitalism, Justice*, 83–89.

INDEX